ROCKY
RIVER
PUBLISHERS

HELP

FOR CHILDREN

FROM INFANCY TO ADULTHOOD

A NATIONAL DIRECTORY OF HOTLINES, HELPLINES, ORGANIZATIONS, AGENCIES, AND OTHER RESOURCES

MIRIAM J. WILLIAMS WILSON, R.N.

ROCKY RIVER PUBLISHERS
P. O. Box 1679
SHEPHERDSTOWN, WV 25443
(304) 876-2711

HELP FOR CHILDREN: From Infancy to Adulthood
5th EDITION

Printing History
First Edition, September, 1987
Second Edition, October, 1987
Third Edition, January, 1988
Fourth Edition, April, 1989
Second Printing, October, 1989
Third Printing, November, 1989
Fifth Edition, September, 1991

Cover design by Jean M. Peterson and Charles William Wilson

ISBN: 0-944576-07-9
Library of Congress Catalog Card Number: 91-062711

Printed in the United States of America
by ARCATA GRAPHICS COMPANY, MARTINSBURG, WV 25401.
Published by ROCKY RIVER PUBLISHERS, Shepherdstown, WV 25443.

Dedicated to:

DR. CHARLES LINDSAY WILSON
my beloved husband and best friend. For nearly 20 years I have had the privilege of sharing my life with you and observing you in your daily life demonstrate love, caring, and helpfulness toward others. You are my personal hero and the wind beneath my wings.

AND
TO OUR CHILDREN

AND
CHILDREN EVERYWHERE

TO THE READER

May I suggest a quick read-through when you first purchase this book. It will help you become acquainted with the scope of services available for our nation's children. You will no doubt be as surprised and delighted as I was to discover a wide variety of services that you never knew existed.

Hundreds of national hotlines, helplines, organizations, clearinghouses, and other support systems—staffed with concerned and loving people—are working to help America's children.

Most of the services are provided free. You will probably find some agencies that you will want to contact right away! A vast network of help and support organizations awaits your call or letter.

Best wishes to you, dear reader, and all those children whose lives you touch. *MJW*

Acknowledgments:

Thank you to all the caring persons who work for the organizations, hotlines, and helplines, who when contacted by phone or letter, gave of your time and skills so generously to contribute to this book.

A very special thank you to Robert Bainum for your concern for children and your help. Despite your extremely busy schedule, you have always taken time to support my work and give me guidance.

Penny and Gerald Wheeler, Richard Coffen, Albert and Reva Kave, Denver Hipp, H. Max Derr, Jo Anne Seems, Lawrence Hitt, Mary Lou and Ed Haynes, Valerie Haynes, Barbara Scott, Cherie Kirk, and Kathy Coston, you have given me a great deal of encouragement through the years. Thank you for being such caring, helpful people in my life.

My deepest appreciation to Eugene Lincoln for taking on the difficult task of copy editing the final manuscript. Also, thank you to Debra L. Wert, Margaret Miller, Dr. Randolph Johnston, Lane Bailey, Barbara Pryor, Jim Fox, and Ramona Remsburg, for your deep concern for children and encouragement.

Sara Niccum, Veronica Ferguson, and Dr. Duan Ragan gave generously of their time to send numerous helpful resources. Many children will be blessed because of their kindness.

I would also like to express my gratitude to Debra McCauley Tokach for her many suggestions of resources for those who daily struggle with the challenge of hearing impairment and visual impairment. Dr. Eugene C. Sheeley also sent some excellent suggestions that will benefit many children.

Thank you Doug Stein, Harold Wright, David Shives, Don Linton, Jerry Wayt, and John Rock. Your kindness has meant a great deal.

Special thanks to Betty Ferguson, Connie Wingfield, Julianne Buckley, Dena Lehman, Karen Warner, Dennis Miller, Dr. Ernestine Ragan, Barbara McRae, Earl Wiehl, and Walt Purdy for your deep concern for children and support of HELP FOR CHILDREN.

Barrie Winnette, Rebecca Winnette-Llewellyn, Rod Llewellyn and Charles William Wilson, Ralph G. Williams, Donald and Georda Williams, Barrie and Mary Anne Williams, Sarah , Jessica, Drs. Ralph and Mary Jane Williams and Mark – you are very special people in my life. Thank you for all your love and encouragement.

Lillian Conn Williams – my wonderful mother. Thank you for filling my childhood with love and for your love and prayers during the many months this book has been in progress. MJW

INTRODUCTION

This book evolved through 29 years of working with child-care professionals, parents, and children. When a crisis would arise or a parent wanted to know where to find help for a particular concern, I found that existing information and resources to help children were scattered and not readily accessible. To compile and have all this valuable information in one easy-to-read volume became a dream of mine. In the fall of 1987 the first edition of HELP FOR CHILDREN was released. It quickly became utilized as a reference throughout the nation. The realization that many children will receive the help that they need and deserve from these wonderful resources has made the preparation of these five editions a very special experience.

I would like to express my appreciation and admiration to all the people behind the associations, clearinghouses, centers, hotlines, helplines, and other support groups who are caring for the needs of our nation's children. Thank you for the generosity, love, and energy that are involved in keeping these services available.

If there are some important resources that I have missed that you think should be included in the next edition, please write to me in care of ROCKY RIVER PUBLISHERS, P.O. Box 1679, Shepherdstown, WV 25443.

Working together, we can help each child sing that unique song—only his or her life can sing—with its full clarity and beauty.

Miriam J. Williams Wilson, R.N.

About the Author

Miriam J. Williams Wilson was born and raised in London, Ontario, Canada. She moved to the United States at the age of eighteen and is now a U.S. citizen. Her professional career spans 29 years. A registered nurse, Mrs. Wilson worked first in charge of an emergency room and later as a head nurse in California. Subsequently she spent four years doing psychiatric testing for a private psychiatric hospital in Ohio and an additional four years as a biofeedback specialist associated with a psychiatrist in Virginia. Two more years were spent directing a Children's Stress Management Center in West Virginia. Since 1987 Mrs. Wilson has been the president of Rocky River Publishers.

Miriam is married to Dr. Charles L. Wilson, a research scientist for the U.S.D.A. Their his, mine, and ours family of eight children are all grown, except for their youngest son Charles Wm. Wilson, age 16, who has assisted in designing several of the covers of HELP FOR CHILDREN to *help* his mom.

Mrs. Wilson is also author of the book:
STRESS STOPPERS FOR CHILDREN AND ADOLESCENTS.

CONTENTS

Chapter 1
CHILD SAFETY

Chapter 2
YOUTH IN DISTRESS

Chapter 3
ABUSED AND MISSING CHILDREN

Chapter 4
CHILDREN'S HEALTH

Chapter 5

CHILDREN'S MENTAL HEALTH AND MENTAL RETARDATION

Chapter 6

CHILDREN WITH DISABILITIES

Chapter 7
MATERNAL AND CHILD CARE

Chapter 8
HELP FOR PARENTS

Chapter 9

INTERNATIONAL CHILDREN'S ORGANIZATIONS

APPENDIX

*** SPECIAL NOTICE - PLEASE READ ***

A few days before the 5th edition of HELP FOR CHILDREN went to press, all the listings were rechecked and phoned to ensure the accuracy of each address and phone number.

Beginning November 2, 1991, approximately half of the current Los Angeles Area Code 213 numbers will be changed to Area Code 310. The 310 Area Code will include the western, coastal, southern and eastern portions of the county, including Los Angeles International Airport. Downtown Los Angeles and some surrounding communities will retain the 213 Area Code. Please note this, and change the numbers in the 213 Area Code that would be affected.

Baltimore, MD and Annapolis, MD, will also be making Area Code changes from Area Code 301 to Area Code 410 in November of 1991.

MJW

"COMPASSION is the chief law of human existence."

DOSTOYEVSKY

1

CHILD SAFETY

CONSUMER PRODUCT SAFETY Our children can be at risk and we may not even be aware of it. Are your children's toys or furniture safe? Does your latchkey child have a safe environment? Is the phone number of your regional poison control center readily available? The following sections will point you toward resources to answer your most important child safety questions.

SAFE TOYS AND FURNITURE

The U. S. Consumer Product Safety Commission can help you with your decisions when buying toys and children's nursery products. They can tell you what toys or other children's products have been recalled. The following free booklets are available: *Crib Safety—Keep Them on the Safe Side*; *Think Toy Safety*; and *Tips for Baby's Safety* (nursery equipment pamphlet both in English and Spanish).
Write: U. S. Consumer Product Safety Commission, Washington, DC 20207 or **Call:** (800) 638-2772.

PRODUCT SAFETY HOTLINE

The Consumer Product Safety Commission provides a hotline on product safety and serves as a contact point for reporting product-related injuries at home, school, or in recreational areas.
Write: Consumer Product Safety Commission, Washington, DC 20207 or **Call:** (800) 638-2772 ; TTY (800) 638-8270.

AMERICAN ACADEMY OF PEDIATRICS PRODUCT RECOMMENDATIONS

An organization concerned with safety issues as they affect your child. It can send you a publication entitled *1991 Family Shopping Guide to Car Seats.*
Write: Family Shopping Guide, American Academy of Pediatrics, P. O. Box 927, Elk Grove Village, IL 60009 (send a self-addressed, stamped envelope).

FIRE SAFETY

Few things are more tragic than a child who has been burned. Many children's lives are lost each year because of poor fire safety practices.

BURN ADVOCACY FOR CHILDREN

The National Burn Victim Foundation has educational programs on burn prevention for schools. Back-to-school programs are available for children who have been scarred/disfigured by burns. An evaluation system, using burn forensics, is available to determine whether a child's burn injury is the result of abuse, neglect, or an accident.
Write: National Burn Victim Foundation, 32-34 Scotland Road, Orange, NJ 07050 or **Call:** (201) 731-3112.

NATIONAL FIRE SAFETY COUNCIL, INC.

Has special fire safety educational programs for fire departments to help save lives. *Firepup*® is the Council's superhero mascot.
Write: National Fire Safety Council, P. O. Box 378, Michigan Center, MI 49254-0378 or **Call:** (517) 764-2811.

COPING WITH MOTHER NATURE

Children may find themselves alone during natural disasters such as floods or earthquakes. It is wise to provide them with some basic survival information.

IN TIME OF EMERGENCY

A free government handbook is available to tell families how to survive in the event of disasters such as fires, floods, hurricanes, tornadoes, winter storms, earthquakes, tidal waves, nuclear power plant accidents, or nuclear attack. The *Big Bird Gets Ready for Hurricanes Kit* sells for $2.25.
Write: Federal Emergency Management Agency, P. O. Box 70274, Washington, DC 20024.

HUG-A-TREE AND SURVIVE

A program to educate children on what to do if they get lost. The group produces a slide show that can be presented by search and rescue or sheriff's reserve personnel.
Write: Hug-A-Tree and Survive, c/o Jacqueline Heet, 6465 Lance Way, San Diego, CA 92120. An all-volunteer organization. Send a self-addressed, stamped envelope when corresponding.

COPING WITH A FLOOD

A free pamphlet entitled *In the Event of a Flood* (564X) tells you what to do during a flood and how to minimize loss of life and property.
Write: Consumer Information Center, Dept. 564X, Pueblo, CO 81009.

COPING WITH AN EARTHQUAKE

A $1.00 booklet *Safety and Survival in an Earthquake* (159X) tells you what to do before, during, and after an earthquake. Learn what to do at home and in your community.
Write: Consumer Information Center, Dept. 159X, Pueblo, CO 81009.

HOME SAFETY The home can present a number of hazards to young people. Below are some potential problems:

BUTTON BATTERY SWALLOWING

Hundreds of instances of button battery swallowing have been reported. Severe injury, permanent damage, and even death can result. Keep batteries from hearing aids, watches, calculators, and electronic games out of the reach of children.

Call: In the event a battery is swallowed, immediately call the National Button Battery Ingestion Hotline collect at (202) 625-3333 or one of the other poison control centers on page 179.

LEAD AND YOUR DRINKING WATER

Lead is very toxic, particularly to children. The EPA has prepared a pamphlet which will tell you how to determine whether you might have a problem with lead in your home water supply and what to do about it. Ask for *Lead and Your Drinking Water* (428X); (Send 50¢).

Write: Consumer Information Center, Dept. 428X, Pueblo, CO 81009.

HAZARDS FROM PESTICIDES

The National Pesticide Telecommunications Network provides information on health hazards of pesticides and safety precautions you can take to protect your child.

Write: NPTN Hotline, Department of Preventive Medicine, Texas Tech University, Lubbock, Texas 79430 or **Call:** (800) 858-7378.

RADON: POTENTIAL HOME HAZARD

Radon gas is colorless, odorless, tasteless – and radioactive. It arises from the breakdown of uranium in rocks and soil, and can accumulate in houses after seeping through cracks in the floors and walls. Prolonged exposure to high levels of radon gas is estimated to cause 5,000 to 20,000 lung cancer deaths a year in the United States. **Write:** Environmental Protection Agency/Radon Division, 401 M Street, S.W., ANR-464, Washington, DC 20460 or **Call:** (800) SOS-RADON.

LATCHKEY SAFETY With both parents working, more young children are being given the responsibilities of handling things at home alone. It is important that you develop a checklist for your child to follow and make plans for possible emergencies. Some valuable resources are available to help you.

CHECKLIST FOR LATCHKEY CHILDREN

The National PTA has developed a checklist to help you make a safer environment for your latchkey child. It can send you information and put you in touch with local projects dealing with latchkey children and their problems.
Write: Project Latchkey, National PTA, 700 North Rush Street, Chicago, IL 60611-9894 or **Call:** (312) 787-0977.

PHONEFRIEND FOR LATCHKEY CHILDREN

The American Association of University Women has published a 200-page "replication packet" for starting and maintaining an after-school call-in line in your community for latchkey children. It costs $22.00 plus $3 for shipping.
Write: Phonefriend, American Association of University Women, P. O. Box 735, State College, PA 16804 or **Call:** (814) 234-9036, ask for Dr. Helen N. Meahl.

PROJECT HOME SAFE

Sponsored by the American Home Economics Association and Whirlpool Foundation, the project has a brochure for parents on finding and assessing school-age child care for school-agers. It provides training and materials to help volunteers and communities develop services for latchkey children and their parents and distributes bibliographies on telephone warm lines, intergenerational programs, school-age child care programs, and related topics.
Write: Project Home Safe, American Home Economic Association, 1555 King Street, Alexandria, VA 22314 or **Call:** (800) 252-SAFE.

PROTECTION FROM INJURY Tragic injuries maim and kill children every day. Proper education of the child and the parent can prevent many of these from occurring.

NATIONAL INJURY INFORMATION CLEARINGHOUSE

A division of the U. S. Consumer Product Safety Commission collects, investigates, analyzes, and disseminates injury data and information relating to the causes and prevention of death, injury, and illness associated with consumer products. The clearinghouse compiles data obtained from accident investigation reports, consumer complaints/reported incidents, death certificates, news clips, and hospitals. **Write:** National Injury Information Clearinghouse, Consumer Product Safety Commission, 5401 Westbard Avenue, Room 625, Washington, DC 20207 or **Call:** (301) 492-6424.

SPECIFIC BRAND NAME INJURY INFORMATION

This office can give you information on specific brand-name products that have caused injury to a child. The request must be in writing. You may contact the following office for further details:
Write: Freedom of Information Office, Consumer Product Safety, 5401 Westbard Avenue, Room 512, Washington, D.C. 20207 or **Call:** (301) 492-5785.

BABY-SITTER RESPONSIBILITIES

If not properly trained or responsible, baby-sitters can pose a threat to children's safety. A free government booklet (meant for baby-sitters) entitled *The Super Sitter* can be obtained from the CPSC. It outlines the responsibilities of a baby-sitter.
Write: U. S. Consumer Product Safety Commission, Washington, DC 20207.

SAFETY PUBLICATIONS

A free catalogue is available on safety-related publications for children. Some of the topics included are playground equipment, poison prevention, toys, and nursery items.

Write: U.S. Consumer Product Safety Commission, Washington, DC 20207 (for single-copy requests).

BOOK ON CHILD SAFETY

A safety book for children is available called *Playing It Safe–Street Smart Activities for Children* ($8.95). It is a complete safety book aimed at the child and parent or guardian. Discussions and activities help the child avoid dangerous situations.

Write: Firefly Books, 250 Sparks Avenue, Willowdale, Ontario, Canada M2H2S4 or **Call:** (416) 499-8412; (FAX) (416) 499-8313.

THE NATIONAL SAFE KIDS CAMPAIGN

The National SAFE KIDS Campaign is a long-term effort to prevent injury, the number-one killer of children. Begun in 1988, it is the first nationwide, comprehensive childhood injury prevention campaign. More than 90 national organizations and 93 state and local coalitions are taking part in the campaign. Former Surgeon General C. Everett Koop, M.D., is chairman of the campaign.

Write: The National SAFE KIDS Campaign, 111 Michigan Avenue, N.W., Washington, DC 20010 or **Call:** (202) 939-4993.

> *"Injury is the leading cause of death among children and young adults. One in 4 injured children will need trauma care."*
>
> **Washington Post,1989**

SAFETY FROM POISONS

Hazardous chemicals and radiation may occur unsuspectedly in a child's environment. We have the responsibility of keeping our children out of harm's way.

POISON CONTROL CENTERS

Your regional poison control center can answer questions about the prevention and treatment of accidents involving the ingestion of poisonous or potentially poisonous substances. **YOU WILL FIND A LISTING OF REGIONAL POISON CONTROL CENTERS ON PAGE 179 IN THE APPENDIX. These centers can provide you and your physician with information on a 24-HOUR basis. Button battery swallowing is dangerous. See special Hotline – pages 20; 179.**

LEAD POISONING

Lead poisoning can be extremely hazardous to you and your family's health. A 50¢ pamphlet titled *What You Should Know About Lead-Based Paint In Your Home* (467X) presents these hazards. It tells how to detect lead in paint, what to do to reduce exposure, and safety guidelines for removing lead-based paint.

Write: Consumer Information Center, Dept. 467X, Pueblo, CO 81009.

FOOD AND DRUG ADMINISTRATION ADVICE

This organization has information on labeling, cosmetics, additives, drugs, quackery, and pregnancy. Pamphlets are available.

Write: Food and Drug Administration, Office of Consumer Affairs, 5600 Fishers Land, Rockville, MD 20857-HFE-88.

REDUCING THE RISK OF FOOD POISONING

The U. S. Department of Agriculture has written a free pamphlet entitled *The Quick Consumer Guide to Safe Food Handling* (574X) which tells you how to reduce the risk of food poisoning. Included are instructions for handling meat and poultry, guidelines for home canning, and what to do when your freezer fails.

Write: Consumer Information Center, Dept. 574X, Pueblo, CO 81009.

TRANSPORTATION SAFETY Tragic accidents often occur to young people while they are in cars, riding bicycles, motorcycles, or in buses. We need to provide them with all the information and protection we can.

AUTO SAFETY HOTLINE

The National Highway Traffic Safety Administration has a toll-free number to answer questions on motor vehicle safety issues, motor vehicle safety recalls, safety defect investigations, new car crash test results, and other safety topics. Operators listed below can also take consumer complaints about possible safety defects as well as assist callers having difficulty obtaining repair work for an existing safety recall.
Write: NHTSA, Auto Safety Hotline, 400 7th Street, S.W., Washington, DC 20590 or **Call:** (800) 424-9393; (202) 366-0123; TTY (800) 434-9153; TTY (202) 755-8919, 8 A.M.– 4 P.M. EST.

OCCUPANT PROTECTION

The National Highway Traffic Safety Administration can provide you with excellent literature for protecting your child in vehicles. Included are: *Car Safety for You and Your Baby* (No. 1P221); *Passenger Protection Laws* (No. 1P805); *Consumer Info: Transporting Your Child Safely* (No. 1P317); *Shopping Guide for Child and Infant Safety Seats* (No. 1P306); and *Protect Your Child With a Child Safety Seat* (No.1P305).
Write: National Highway Traffic Safety Administration, Office of Occupant Protection, NTS-13, 400 7th Street, S.W., Washington, DC 20590.

SAFETY BELTS IN SCHOOL BUSES

A publication which discusses the use of seat belts in school buses is available from the National Head Injury Foundation. Ask for *Safety Belts in School Buses* ($4.00).
Write: National Head Injury Foundation, 333 Turnpike Road, Southborough, MA 01772 or **Call:** (508) 485-9950; (800) 444-NHIF (for families of injured only).

"BUCKLE UP" CLUBS AND GAMES

Free coloring books, games, club memberships, and posters centered around "Vince & Larry" are available from the National Highway Safety Administration. A foldout teaching module for grades K-6 includes a 16 x 20-inch board game and other student activities. "Vince & Larry Buckle Up for Life Club" membership cards are available. Also they provide one-inch stickers of a red heart wearing a safety belt with the words, "We Love You – Buckle Up!", 36 stickers per sheet.
Write: National Highway Traffic Safety Administration, NTS-13, Office of Occupant Protection, 400 7th Street, S.W., Washington, DC 20590.

PREVENT PEDESTRIAN ACCIDENTS

Children are very vulnerable as pedestrians. The National Highway Traffic Safety Administration can send you a two-sided sheet that describes common myths children have about being pedestrians (Item IP304). It also contains a message for parents of preschool children.
Write: National Highway Traffic Safety Administration, NTS-23, 400 7th Street, S.W., Washington, DC 20590 or **Call:** (202) 366-2696.

PREVENTING BICYCLE ACCIDENTS

The National Highway Traffic Safety Administration can send you a two-sided sheet that will help you teach your child how to ride a bike safely. Ask for *How to Ride A Bike* (1P313).
Write: National Highway Traffic Safety Administration, NTS-23, 400 7th Street, S.W., Washington, DC 20590 or **Call:** (202) 366-2696.

HELMETS FOR BICYCLE RIDERS

Over 400,000 children are sent to emergency rooms each year, and 600 die because of bicycle accidents. Most deaths come from head injuries which could have been avoided if the child had been wearing a helmet. The American Academy of Pediatrics offers a free brochure which includes a coupon for buying a $45 child's helmet for $16.95. For a copy send a self-addressed, stamped envelope.
Write: American Academy of Pediatrics, Bicycle Helmet Brochure, 141 Northwest Point Blvd., Elk Grove Village, IL 60009.

ALCOHOL AND SAFETY Drinking and driving are a deadly combination. The aftermath may leave a child severely injured or killed. We must prevent these tragedies from occurring.

ALCOHOL AND DRIVING PROGRAMS

The National Highway Traffic Safety Administration can provide a number of free publications and educational flyers on alcohol and youthful drivers. Included are: *An Improved Driver Entry System for Young Novice Drivers* (No. 2P321); *Be Smart. Do Your Part. Don't Start* (No. 2P632); and *Determinants of Youth Attitudes and Skills for DWI Prevention Programs* (No. 2P301). *A Life of the Party Pack* (No. 2P132) offers the host or hostess practical suggestions to help their guests enjoy the party and still be able to drive home safely. Fifteen tasty non-alcoholic drink recipes are included.
Write: National Highway Traffic Safety Administration, Alcohol Program, NTS-20, 400 7th Street, S.W., Washington, DC 20590.

STUDENTS AGAINST DRIVING DRUNK (SADD)

This organization attempts to develop better communication between parents and the teenager. It can send you a contract that the parent and teenager can sign, stating that the teenager will always call the parent and that the parent will always respond. The contract is a *no-use* message between the teenager and the parent. The young person will work to eliminate underage drinking, drug abuse, and to end death due to drinking and driving.
Write: SADD, P. O. Box 800, Marlboro, MA 01752 or **Call:** (508) 481-3568.

"There is more to life than increasing its speed."

Gandhi

MOTHERS AGAINST DRUNK DRIVING (MADD)

The mission of Mothers Against Drunk Driving is to stop drunk driving and to support victims of this violent crime. MADD's over 400 chapters have a wide array of literature for victims, most offer victim support groups, and all chapters have victim advocates.
Write: Mothers Against Drunk Driving, National Office, 511 E. John Carpenter Freeway, Suite 700, Irving, TX 75062 or **Call:** (800) GET-MADD; (214) 744-6233.

REMOVE INTOXICATED DRIVERS (RID-USA)

The oldest anti-drunk driving organization in the U. S. Provides free help and information to victims of drunk drivers and other alcohol-related crises. It publishes a quarterly newsletter and bulletins.
Write: RID-USA, P. O. Box 520, Schenectady, NY 12301 or **Call:** Hotline (518) 372-0034 (24 hours, 7 days a week); or (518) 372-9624.

PARENT GUIDE FOR A SAFE GRADUATION

The graduation season with its parties can result in numerous teenage accidents on the highways. The Washington Regional Alcohol Program can send you a brochure entitled *A Parent's Guide to a Safe Graduation,* which contains tips on how to avoid those accidents.
Write: Washington Regional Alcohol Programs, Box 150489, Chevy Chase, MD 20815 or **Call:** (301) 565-4161.

ATHLETES AGAINST DRINKING

A free manual, *Road to Winning,* is available from the National Highway Traffic Safety Administration. It uses professional athletes and college athletes to promote highway safety programs for high school students. It lists the program objectives, program format, giving sample opening remarks for talks before students. Also, it gives sample remarks for athletes who address the students about safe driving.
Write: National Highway Safety Administration, Alcohol Programs, 400 7th Street, S. W., Washington, DC 20590.

SAFETY FROM VIOLENCE There are precautions that you can take to reduce the risks of violence to your child in the home, at school, and on the streets. The following information should prove useful to you:

PROTECTING YOUR FAMILY AGAINST CRIME

The FBI can provide you and your family a booklet entitled *Crime Resistance – A Way To Protect Your Family Against Crime*. It presents ways to protect your family in and out of the home and while traveling, walking, or shopping.
Write: Office of Public Affairs, Room 6236, Federal Bureau of Investigation, 10th Street and Pennsylvania Avenue, N.W., Washington, DC 20535.

NATIONAL SCHOOL SAFETY CENTER

An organization at Pepperdine University serves as a national clearinghouse on school crime and violence. It can provide training and technical assistance to school districts, law enforcement agencies, professional organizations, and citizens nationwide.
Write: National School Safety Center, Pepperdine University, Malibu, CA 90263 or **Call:** (818) 377-6200.

NATIONAL CHILD SAFETY COUNCIL

The Council provides safety educational materials to law-enforcement agencies and schools nationwide. NCSC introduced/created the missing-children programs on milk cartons, grocery bags, and with utilities across the country, and displays these pictures nationwide. *Safetypup®* is the Council's superhero mascot.
Write: National Child Safety Council, P. O. Box 1368, Jackson, MI 49204-1368 or **Call:** (517) 764-6070.

> *"When analyzed by age group, 82 percent of the 3- to 9-year-olds, 66 percent of the 10- to 14-year-olds, and 34 percent of the 15- to 17-year-olds had been victims of some form of violence during the year."* HHS

COLLEGE KILLINGS

Violence is an increasing problem on college campuses. Hazings by high school and college campus organizations sometimes include life-threatening violent acts. An organization directed toward halting violence during hazings can be contacted for information.

Write: Committee to Halt Useless College Killings (C.H.U.C.K.), P. O. Box 188, Sayville, NY 11782 or **Call:** (516) 567-1130.

HATE VIOLENCE

A national clearinghouse monitors hate groups throughout the U. S. that promote violence. It provides victim assistance, leadership training, and education.

Write: Center for Democratic Renewal, P. O. Box 50469, Atlanta, GA 30302 or (404) 221-0025.

PREJUDICE AND VIOLENCE

The National Institute Against Prejudice and Violence provides consultation and training on victimization to law enforcement personnel, victim assistance providers, and community organizations.

Write: National Institute Against Prejudice and Violence, 31 South Greene Street, Baltimore, MD 21201 or **Call:** (301) 328-5170.

DEALING WITH CULTS

Young people can sometime enter destructive relationships with cults. Counsel and information is available through two cult information clearinghouses.

Write: American Family Foundation, Box 2265, Bonita Springs, FL 33959 or **Call:** (212) 249-7693.

Write: Cult Awareness Network, 2421 W. Pratt Boulevard, Suite 1173, Chicago, IL 60645 or **Call:** (312) 267-7777.

> *"Never open the door to a lesser evil, for other and greater ones invariably slink in after it."*
>
> Battosoe Gracian

ASSISTANCE FOR VICTIMS Victims are often very vulnerable and need assistance immediately. Unfortunately, many children and women are victimized in their own homes. A number of organizations and hotlines can give you the help you need.

NATIONAL VICTIMS RESOURCE CENTER

NVRC is a national clearinghouse for victim-related information funded by the Office for Victims of Crime, U.S. Department of Justice. It has more than 7,000 victim-related books and articles covering child physical and sexual abuse, victims services, domestic violence, victim-witness programs, and violent crime. Information is available on state victim compensation programs funded by the Office for Victims of Crime.

Write: U.S. Department of Justice, Office of Justice Programs, Office for Victims of Crime, Box 6000, Rockville, MD 20850 or **Call:** (301) 251-5500; (800) 627-6872 (NVRC); Electronic Bulletin Board is available.

RESOURCES FOR VICTIMS

The primary purpose of the Office for Victims of Crime is to provide financial assistance to the states for the purpose of compensating and otherwise assisting victims of crime and to provide funds for the purpose of assisting victims of federal crime.

Write: Office for Victims of Crime, Department of Justice, Room 1352, 633 Indiana Avenue, N.W., Washington, DC 20531 or **Call:** (800) 627-6872; (202) 307-5947.

NATIONAL COALITION AGAINST DOMESTIC VIOLENCE NCADV develops materials that speak to the needs of battered women and their children. Distributes publications, including a national shelter directory; provides speakers on topics related to domestic violence; provides technical assistance, including a special project for children.

Write: NCADV, P.O. Box 34103, Washington, DC 20043-4103 or **Call:** (202) 638-6388; TTY (202) 589-6671.

HOTLINE AGAINST DOMESTIC VIOLENCE
A national 24-hour hotline number can be called which makes referrals to 1,200 domestic violence shelters in the U. S.
Write: Michigan Coalition Against Domestic Violence, P. O. Box 7032, Huntington Woods, MI 48070 or **Call:** (800) 333-7233.

NATIONAL ORGANIZATION FOR VICTIM ASSISTANCE (NOVA) NOVA exists to help victims of crime and other stark misfortunes. Provides direct services to victims, and has victim advocates and referrals to programs elsewhere in the country. Publications are available. **Write:** National Organization for Victim Assistance (NOVA), 1757 Park Road, N.W., Washington, DC 20010 or **Call:** (202) 232-6682 (24-hour hotline).

NATIONAL COUNCIL ON CHILD ABUSE AND FAMILY VIOLENCE Provides referrals through its national toll-free helpline to children, women, and the elderly who are victims of violence.
Write: National Council on Child Abuse and Family Violence, 1155 Connecticut Avenue, N.W., Suite 300, Washington, DC 20036 or **Call:** (800) 222-2000; (202) 429-6695.

CALIFORNIA CENTER ON VICTIMOLOGY
Assists victims of crime throughout court process and after, legal clinic advocates, counseling for victims, media advocacy, and legislation. "It's a F.A.C.T. (Families Affected by Crime and Trauma)" program is designed to help children as secondary victims with counseling services.
Write: California Center on Victimology, 11221 22nd Street, San Diego, CA 92102 or **Call:** (619) 235-4459.

SUPPORT FOR CHILDREN OF PRISONERS

Parents and Children Together is an organization working to help the children of prisoners. A free booklet is available about how the incarceration of a parent affects a child.

Write: PACT (Parents and Children Together), P. O. Box 15543, Fort Worth, TX 76119 or **Call:** (817) 531-1469.

PARENTS OF MURDERED CHILDREN AND OTHER SURVIVORS OF HOMICIDE VICTIMS

This is a self-help organization for those people who have lost a loved one to murder. It conducts support-group meetings and provides additional assistance through published materials, court advocacy, and on a one-to-one basis over the phone and through the mail.

Write: POMC, 100 E. 8th Street, Cincinnati, OH 45202 or **Call:** (513) 721-5683.

> *"The ultimate weakness of violence is it is a descending spiral...instead of diminishing evil, it multiplies it."*
>
> Martin Luther King, Jr. 1967

2

YOUTH IN DISTRESS

ALCOHOL ABUSE Drugs are receiving most of the attention in regard to substance abuse among our teenagers. However, alcohol abuse is just as pressing a problem. A number of groups are standing by to help schools or individuals deal with alcohol abuse.

ALCOHOL CLEARINGHOUSE

You can address your questions on alcohol and children to a national clearinghouse. It can put you in touch with effective programs to prevent alcohol abuse by teenagers.
Write: National Clearinghouse for Alcohol Information (NCALI), P. O. Box 2345, Rockville, MD 20852 or **Call:** (800) 729-6686; (301) 468-2600.

ALCOHOLICS ANONYMOUS

This renowned organization can send you a catalog listing books, pamphlets, and audiovisual materials describing the twelve-step program of recovery. Some are free, and others are available at listed prices. It can also put you in touch with local help.
Write: Alcoholics Anonymous, P. O. Box 459, Grand Central Station, New York, NY 10163 or **Call:** (212) 686-1100.

SUPPORT GROUPS FOR FAMILIES AND FRIENDS OF ALCOHOLICS

An alcoholic in the family affects all its members. Fortunately, others dealing with this problem are willing to share their experience and support.

ALATEEN

A fellowship of young Al-Anon members, usually teenagers, whose lives have been affected by someone else's drinking.
Write: Al-Anon Family Group Headquarters, Inc., P. O. Box 862, Midtown Station, New York, NY 10018-0862 or **Call:** (800) 356-9996; (212) 302-7240.

AL-ANON

A worldwide organization that offers a self-help recovery program for families and friends of alcoholics whether or not the alcoholic seeks help or even recognizes the existence of a drinking problem. Members give and receive comfort and understanding through a mutual exchange of experiences. A catalog of literature, films, tapes, and kits is available upon request.
Write: Al-Anon Family Group Headquarters, Inc., P. O. Box 862, Midtown Station, New York, NY 10018-0862 or **Call:** (800) 356-9996; (212) 302-7240.

CHILDREN OF ALCOHOLICS

Children of alcoholics have special problems. A number of self-help organizations can put you in touch with information and concerned people who want to help.
Write: The National Association for Children of Alcoholics, 31582 Coast Highway, Suite B, South Laguna, CA 92677 or **Call:** (714) 499-3889.
Write: Children of Alcoholics Foundation, Inc., P. O. Box 4185, Grand Central Station, New York, NY 10163.
Write: Suzanne Somers Institute (for the Effects of Addictions on Families), P. O. Box 16502, Irvine, CA 92713.

ALCOHOL PROBLEMS IN ELEMENTARY SCHOOL

Children experience pressure to experiment with alcohol and other drugs while still in elementary school. This pressure can exist as early as the fourth grade. A collection of educational material aimed at educating the elementary student about alcohol problems can be obtained at a modest price from the NCADI.

Write: National Clearinghouse for Alcohol and Drug Information, P. O. Box 2345, Rockville, MD 20852 or **Call:** (301) 468-2600; (800) 729-6686; (800) SAY-NO-TO; TDD (800) 487-4889.

ALCOHOL AND DRUG ABUSE

A variety of educational programs exists which can assist teachers and parents as they try to instruct children on how to avoid the pitfalls of drug and alcohol abuse.

ALCOHOL AND DRUGS IN THE SCHOOLS

Target – Helping students cope with alcohol, tobacco, and other drugs is an organization that serves as a resource center for information on chemical abuse for students from preschool to the 12th grade. It provides, through the National Federation of State High School Associations, ways to educate students to develop and continue healthy lifestyles.

Write: Target, P. O. Box 20626, 11724 N.W. Plaza Circle, Kansas City, MO 64195-0626 or **Call:** (800) 366-6667; (816) 464-5400.

GROWING UP DRUG FREE

A free publication *Growing Up Drug Free* (551X) is available that shows what children should understand about drugs, including alcohol and tobacco, at each age level. It identifies classes and types of drugs, and resource contacts.

Write: Consumer Information Center, Dept. 551X, Pueblo, CO 81009.

> *Almost 20 percent of teens between 14 and 17 are problem drinkers, according to the American Health Foundation.*

DRUG ABUSE We are all aware of the destruction that drugs are causing among our young people. Perhaps you are not as aware of the organizations and resources which are attacking this problem.

DRUG-ABUSE INFORMATION

The National Clearinghouse on Drug Abuse and Alcohol. For information: **Call:** (301) 468-2600; and for drug-abuse treatment and referral: **Call:** (800) 662-HELP (days, weekends, evenings); (800) 729-6686 (National Clearinghouse).

CONFIDENTIAL COCAINE REFERRAL LINE

The U. S. Department of Health and Human Services maintains a confidential information and referral hotline (called National Institute on Drug Abuse [NIDA] Hotline) that directs callers to cocaine-abuse treatment centers in their local communities. Free materials on drug abuse are also distributed in response to inquiries. Refers those using drugs and family members of users to counseling.

Call: (800) 662-HELP (9 a. m.–3 a.m. EST, Mon.-Fri. and 12 noon–3 a.m. EST, Sat. and Sun.). Can send a package of literature on cocaine, marijuana, and alcohol abuse. For literature in bulk **Call:** National Clearinghouse of Alcohol and Drug Information (800) 629-6686.

THE HEALTH CONNECTION

This is a nonprofit organization that has been developing and distributing drug-prevention materials for almost forty years. Two excellent monthly classroom publications, *The Winner* for grades 4–6 or ages 8–12 and *Listen* for teenagers, are available. These publications are designed to motivate children to choose a drug-free lifestyle. A free catalog will be sent on request.

Write: The Health Connection, Narcotics Education, Inc., 55 West Oak Ridge Drive, Hagerstown, MD 21740-7390 or **Call:** (800) 548-8700; (301) 790-9735.

COMMITTEES OF CORRESPONDENCE

A national organization whose purpose is to expose the drug culture and challenge it where and when needed. It identifies the best and worst in drug information. Provides a newsletter and action alert notices with accurate information to help concerned citizens keep abreast of what is happening. It has a national and international network.
Write: Committees of Correspondence, Inc., 57 Conant Street, Room 113, Danvers, MA 01923 or **Call:** (508) 774-2641.

THE AMERICAN COUNCIL FOR DRUG EDUCATION

Among the council's projects are over fifty pamphlets and monographs, four films, and other teaching aids on the health risks associated with using marijuana, cocaine, alcohol, and other widely abused psychoactive drugs. The council will assist educators, parents, and industry leaders in their efforts to address drug-use problems.
Write: The American Council for Drug Education, 204 Monroe Street, Rockville, MD 20850 or **Call:** (301) 294-0600.

COCAINE HELPLINE

A 24-hour information and referral service available for abusers of cocaine. Reformed cocaine addict counselors answer the phones, offering guidance and referring drug users and parents to local public and private treatment centers and family learning centers.
Call: (800) COCAINE.

According to The National Council on Alcoholism over half of all teenage deaths are associated with alcohol or drug usage.

PARENTS AGAINST DRUG ABUSE Parents are on the front line in the fight against drug abuse among our teenagers. They need all the help they can get. Fortunately, several organizations stand ready to give assistance.

PARENTS' RESOURCE INSTITUTE FOR DRUG EDUCATION (PRIDE) A national resource and information center, Parent's Resource Institute for Drug Education (PRIDE) refers concerned parents to groups in their state or local area, gives information on how parents can form a drug-abuse prevention group in their community, and provides telephone consulting and referrals to emergency health centers.
Write: National Parents' Resource Institute for Drug Education, Inc., 50 Hurt Plaza, Suite 210, Atlanta, GA 30303 or **Call:**(404) 577-4500.

PARENTS FOR DRUG-FREE YOUTH
The National Federation of Parents for Drug-Free Youth has over 8,000 local chapters and serves as a clearinghouse and referral agency on youth drug- and alcohol-abuse problems. Brochures are available entitled, *What Parents Must Learn About Teens and Marijuana* and *What Parents Need To Know About Teens and Cocaine* (single copies are free, minimum charge for multiple copies). You can purchase training called REACH (Responsible Educated Adolescents Can Help). A Community Team Manual, and a Drug Prevention Curriculum Guide and Red Ribbon Handbook are available.
Write: National Federation of Parents for Drug-Free Youth, P.O. Box 3878, St. Louis, MO 63122 or **Call:**(314) 968-1322.

"Approximately two out of three teenagers will experiment with illicit drugs."
Youth and Exploitation

REACH AMERICA (NATIONAL FEDERATION OF PARENTS FOR DRUG FREE YOUTH, INC.)

REACH America is the nation's largest secondary school drug-prevention training program. It is a partnership between the National Federation of Parents for Drug Free Youth, Inc., the local community, and the trained students. Instead of simply educating students about drugs, REACH America recruits student volunteers to educate elementary school students.

Write: NFP REACH America, P. O. Box 3412, Albuquerque, NM 87190-3412 or **Call:** (505) 345-7134.

DRUG PROGRAMS FOR NATIVE HAWAIIANS

Special assistance can be obtained in drug-prevention education for native Hawaiian youth. The program is administered by KS/BE in cooperation with the Office of the Governor of Hawaii and the Hawaii State Department of Education.

Write: Native Hawaiian Drug Free Schools and Communities Program,c/o Kanehameha Schools/Bernice Pauahi Bishop Estate, Kapalama Heights, Honolulu, Hawaii 96817 or **Call:** (808) 842-5802.

C. E. MENDEZ FOUNDATION, INC.

Provides comprehensive drug-prevention education for children in grades K-12 and their parents. Training and materials are offered as part of these programs. The foundation offers an after-school activities program titled *On the Right Track* for children ages 5-12. Mendez is also the publisher of the book *Teenagers, Drugs and Growing Up* by Dr. Gary DuDell, which is designed as a handbook on drug prevention for parents and adults involved with adolescents.

Write: C. E. Mendez Foundation, Inc., P. O. Box 10059, Tampa, FL 33679 or **Call:** (813) 251-3600.

NATIONAL FAMILIES IN ACTION

A nationwide volunteer movement to prevent drug abuse in families and communities. Its purpose is to educate society about the dangers of drug abuse by disseminating accurate information and empowering citizens to work for change.
Write: National Families in Action, 2296 Henderson Mill Road, Suite 204, Atlanta, GA 30345 or **Call:** (404) 934-6364.

COMMUNITY INTERVENTION, INC.

Can provide educational material and training programs on drug abuse for young people. Has free publications entitled *Saying Yes, Saying No* and *Adolescent Drug and Alcohol Use: Signs and Symptoms*. Publishes a newspaper that addresses adolescent alcohol and drug issues that is available free of charge. Write for free catalog.
Write: Community Intervention, Inc., 529 S. Seventh Street, Suite 570, Minneapolis, MN 55415 or **Call:** (800) 328-0417; (612) 332-6537.

VETERANS AGAINST DRUGS

A coalition of 26 national veterans organizations united in the war on illegal drugs. It promotes the involvement of veterans and veteran's organizations in anti-drug programs in their communities.
Write: Veterans Against Drugs, 1219 Prince Street, Alexandria, VA 22314 or **Call:** (800) 487-1970; (703) 519-7009.

DRUG PROGRAMS FOR INDIAN YOUTH

Special assistance can be obtained in drug-prevention education for Indian youth. The program is co-administered with the Drug Free Schools Program.
Write: Drug Free Schools Program, Office of Indian Education Program, Bureau of Indian Affairs, MS 3530-MIB-Code 521, 1849 C Street, N.W., Washington, DC 20240 or **Call:** (202) 219-1129.

> *"Faults are thick where love is thin."*
> **James Howell**

DRUGS IN THE SCHOOLS

Young people often receive their first exposure to drugs in our schools. We must fortify our children to resist the temptations presented them to use drugs. Excellent educational programs are available to prevent drug abuse.

KEEPING DRUGS OUT OF THE SCHOOLS

A free guide is available for parents, schools, students, and communities on how to fight drug use by children. It describes the extent of the problem, effects of various drugs, and signs of use. Also included are legal considerations and an extensive list of resources. The title of the publication is *Schools Without Drugs* (553X).
Write: Consumer Information Center, Dept. 553X, Pueblo, CO 81009.

RECOGNITION FOR DRUG-FREE SCHOOL PROGRAMS

The Department of Education has a competitive evaluation and award program to identify and recognize public and private elementary and secondary schools implementing comprehensive prevention programs which have succeeded in reducing student substance abuse.
Write: Drug-Free Schools Recognition Program, Department of Education, Room 508, CP, 555 New Jersey Avenue, N.W., Washington, DC 20208-5645 or **Call:** (202) 219-2134.

TOP-RATED BOOKS IN DRUG EDUCATION FOR ELEMENTARY-AGE CHILDREN

A leading drug educator wrote "I have been working in the drug prevention field for nearly 10 years and during these 10 years there has not been a publication like MAC'S CHOICE that has excited me like this book....The book is wonderful." Now being used in classrooms in over 120 major school systems. The teachers love the ease of use and children are spellbound with the story. Parents love to read and reread it to their children. MAC'S CHOICE ($8.95); MAC'S CHOICE WORKBOOK ($3.50). Write for a free catalog.
Write: Rocky River Publishers, P.O. Box 1679, Shepherdstown, WV 25443 or **Call:** (304) 876-2711; (800) 343-0686 (for book orders only).

COACHES' PROGRAM FOR DRUG PREVENTION

The National High School Athletic Coaches Association sponsors a program to assist coaches in preventing drug and alcohol abuse among young people. Coaches can receive free information on drug and alcohol problems and prevention. Clinics and workshops on drug prevention are conducted for coaches by Federal Drug Enforcement Administration agents and professional and amateur athletes.

Write: Demand Reduction Section, Drug Enforcement Administration, Washington, DC 20537 or **Call:** (202) 307-7936.

JUST SAY NO FOUNDATION

Provides an educational and recreational substance-abuse prevention program for children ages 7-14 by promoting the establishment of peer support groups. Helps in the formation of "Just Say No" Clubs.

Write: Just Say No Foundation, 1777 North California Boulevard, Suite 210, Walnut Creek, CA 94596 or **Call:** (800) 258-2766. In California (415) 939-6666.

YOUTH TO YOUTH

A drug/alcohol-prevention program for teens. The focus is on harnessing the powerful force of peer pressure, often turning it around to become a positive force that encourages young people to live alcohol- and drug-free lives. The program provides leadership training and self-esteem building through conferences and workshops and promotes exciting drug-free events.

Write: Youth to Youth, Sharon McCloy Reichard, 700 Bryden Road, 3rd Floor, Columbus, OH 43215 or **Call:** (614) 224-4506.

DRUG-EDUCATION INFORMATION

Free drug-education material is available from the Department of Justice for civic, educational, private, and religious groups.

Write: Office of Public Affairs, Drug Enforcement Administration, Department of Justice, 1405 I Street, N.W., Room 1209, Washington, DC 20537 or **Call:** (202) 633-1469.

SUPPORT GROUPS/DRUG-TREATMENT PROGRAMS

SUPPORT GROUPS/DRUG-TREATMENT PROGRAMS Strength lies in numbers, particularly when families must deal with the difficulties posed where a family member uses drugs. Fortunately, numerous groups and organizations exist which can give support when it is needed.

NAR-ANON FAMILY GROUP

National self-help group organized to assist families dealing with drug- abuse problems.
Write: Nar-Anon Family Group Headquarters, Inc., P. O. Box 2562, Palos Verdes Peninsula, CA 90274 or **Call:** (213) 547-5800.

HAZELDEN FOUNDATION

A number of services are provided for chemical dependency and other addictive behaviors, including a rehabilitation center, a treatment center, and programs for adolescents and young adults. Has inpatient and outpatient treatment, as well as live-in programs. Pamphlets and audiovisual materials are available.
Write: Hazelden, Box 11, Center City, MN 55012-0011 or **Call:** (612) 257-4010.

STRAIGHT, INC.

Has an intensive, highly structured program to rehabilitate young drug users. It requires 9 to 12 months and involves the drug user and his/her family. Publishes reprints and videotapes.
Write: Straight, Inc., 3001 Gandy Blvd., St. Petersburg, FL 33702 or **Call:** (813) 576-8929.

TOUGHLOVE

National self-help group united to help parents with children who are demonstrating inappropriate behavior.
Write: Toughlove, P. O. Box 1069, Doylestown, PA 18901 or **Call:** (800) 333-1069; (215) 348-7090.

NICOTINE ADDICTION Even though tobacco has been shown to be clearly related to a number of illnesses, including cancer, young people still are becoming addicted to this habit.

OFFICE OF SMOKING AND HEALTH

The Public Health Service can provide information on all aspects of tobacco and its effects, methods of ingestion, and prevention and treatment programs.

Write: Public Health Services, Technical Information Center, Park Building, 5600 Fishers Lane, Rockville, MD 20857 or **Call:** (301) 443-1690.

HOW TO STOP SMOKING

A publication, *How to Stop Smoking Without Gaining Weight*, graphically shows what smoking does to the body. It illustrates the effects of smoking on the lungs, arteries, and brain. Also shows how you can stop smoking without gaining weight. Cost is $2.25.

Write: Review and Herald Publishing Association, 55 West Oak Ridge Drive, Hagerstown, MD 21740.

ANABOLIC STEROIDS The lure of excelling in athletics and looking more attractive has caused a number of young people to use anabolic steroids. Young people must become aware of the potentially dangerous side effects of these drugs.

SIDE EFFECTS OF ANABOLIC STEROIDS

Anabolic steroids are popular muscle-building drugs which can harm your child. The Food and Drug Administration has developed a free pamphlet entitled *Anabolic Steroids: Losing at Winning* (504X) that discusses the dangerous side effects and reactions to these drugs.

Write: Consumer Information Center, Dept. 504X, Pueblo, Colorado 81009.

RUNAWAYS

Teenagers need our help. Fortunately, society is becoming more aware of teenage problems with drugs, alcohol, suicide, and pregnancy. Also, better communication systems are available to help runaways and their families. Following are some of the more outstanding programs and sources of information:

RUNAWAY HOTLINE

National Runaway Switchboard and Suicide Hotline for youth. It can provide help for both parents and youths.
Call: (800) 621-4000 (24 hours a day).

DIRECTORY OF RUNAWAY PROGRAMS

A free national directory of runaway youth programs is available from the Department of Health and Human Services.
Write: Family and Youth Services Bureau, Administration on Children, Youth and Families, Department of Health and Human Services, P. O. Box 1182, Washington, DC 20013 or **Call:** (202) 245-0102.

RUNAWAY HOTLINE

A 24-hour hotline is maintained to promote communication between parents and runaways, who do not have to divulge their location. The Runaway Hotline will make referrals to shelters, and counseling, transportation, medical, and legal services.
Call: (800) 231-6946. In Texas (800) 392-3352.

> *"The common estimate is that 1.2 million to 1.5 million children and adolescents, ages ten through seventeen, run away from home each year in the United States."*
>
> **Children's Defense Fund, 1989**

CRISIS CENTERS AND LONG-TERM SHELTERS

A caring haven for distressed teenagers can sometimes be the only escape that they may have from a life on the streets. A number of these shelters exist throughout the country:

COVENANT HOUSE

An organization that shelters and cares for runaway, homeless kids—over 1,000 daily. CH maintains a national NINELINE with counselors standing by to respond to kids and parents in need 24 hours a day.
Write: Covenant House, P. O. Box 731, Times Square Station, New York, NY 10108-9999 or **Call:** (800) 999-9999; (212) 330-0469.

YOUTH HAVEN IN FLORIDA

Youth Haven in Florida has as its primary purpose providing emergency, temporary shelter and long-term care of abused, abandoned, neglected, and troubled children from birth to age 18.
Write: Youth Haven, Inc., P. O. Box 7007, Naples, FL 33941 or **Call:** (813) 774-2904; (813) 774-2698.

NEUTRAL GROUND FOR TEENAGERS IN KANSAS

Wyandotte House/Neutral Ground in Kansas City can provide long- or short-term crisis intervention for teenagers. Emergency and residential shelter is available for abused, deprived, and neglected children (birth to 17 years).
Write: Wyandotte House/Neutral Ground, Wyandotte House, Inc., 632 Tauromee, Kansas City, KS 66101 or **Call:** (913) 342-9332.

PROSTITUTION AND PORNOGRAPHY

Children of the Night provides protection and support for children, 8-17, who are involved in pornography or prostitution. Operates an outreach program and 24-hour toll-free statewide hotline with a 24-hour bed shelter.
Write: Children of the Night, P. O. Box 4343, Hollywood, CA 90078 or **Call:** (818) 908-4470; CA Hotline (800) 564-COTN.

TEENAGE PREGNANCY Many young people experience much suffering at an early age because of sexual promiscuity or rape. We need to do a better job of educating our teenagers about their sexuality and how to protect themselves against sexual assault.

ADOLESCENT PREGNANCY

Federal programs and funding concerning adolescent pregnancy are administered by a division of the Public Health Service. The PHS can provide you with up-to-date information on this subject.
Write: Office of Adolescent Pregnancy Programs, U.S. Department of Health and Human Services, 200 Independence Avenue, S.W., Room 736 E., Washington, DC 20201 **Call:** (202) 245-7473. Also, **Write:** Family Life Information Exchange, P. O. Box 37299, Washington, DC 20013-7299 or **Call:** (301) 585-6636.

ADOLESCENT PREGNANCY PREVENTION CLEARINGHOUSE

The Children's Defense Fund publishes six reports a year in a subscription series on preventing children from having children. Single issues are $4.50 (including first-class postage).
Write: Children's Defense Fund, 122 C Street, N.W., Washington, DC 20001 or **Call:** (202) 628-8787.

REDUCE UNINTENDED PREGNANCIES

Free booklets on how to prevent unintended pregnancies. Aimed at males, young teenagers, and parents. *Straight Facts for Men About Sex, The Facts,* and *A Parent's Guide to the Facts.* Send a stamped, self-addressed business-size envelope for each to the ACOG.
Write: American College of Obstetricians and Gynecologists, Public Information, 409 12th Street, S.W., Washington, DC 20024-2188.

> *"We want far better reasons for having children than not knowing how to prevent them."*
>
> Dora Russell

BIRTH CONTROL Individuals and organizations differ in their counsel to young people concerning birth control. Nevertheless, it is important that our youth receive competent counsel.

CONTRACEPTIVE USE

The government publishes a free eight-page fact sheet entitled *Contraception: Comparing the Options* (527X). It lists and evaluates the nine common methods of birth control.
Write: Consumer Information Center, Dept. 527X, Pueblo, CO 81009.

CONDOMS AND AIDS

A free booklet *Condoms and Sexually Transmitted Diseases ... Especially AIDS* (571X) helps you understand why it's important to use condoms (rubbers, prophylactics) to help reduce the spread of sexually transmitted diseases. These diseases include AIDS, chlamydia, genital herpes, genital warts, gonorrhea, hepatitis B, and syphilis.
Write: Consumer Information Center, Dept. 571X, Pueblo, CO 81009.

TEENS-HELPING-TEENS PHONELINE

This organization has information on developing teens-helping-teens phone lines. It is working toward a better understanding of the dynamics and consequences of teen sex and pregnancy.
Write: Lee County Youth Services, 112 Hillcrest Drive, P. O. Box 57, Sanford, NC 27330 or **Call:** (919) 774-9515.

> *"Every year, 1.1 million American teens become pregnant. Babies born to school-age mothers run a greater risk of dying before their first birthday."*
>
> **Washington Post, 1989**

VENEREAL DISEASES

Although AIDS is receiving most of the attention, other venereal diseases are still taking a major toll among our teenagers. People are available to give emergency help and counsel.

SEXUALLY TRANSMITTED DISEASE HOTLINE

A national hotline exists that will provide callers with information on sexually transmitted diseases. STD can refer you to public clinics, medical societies, and crisis lines throughout the U.S. Provides written information about sexually transmitted diseases and their prevention. A number of pamphlets are available in English and Spanish on AIDS, genital warts, and chlamydia prevention.
Call: STD National Hotline (800) 227-8922 (Monday through Friday 8-11 pm, EST).

NATIONAL HERPES HOTLINE

Can provide you with a wide variety materials, including a quarterly newsletter, pamphlets, audio and video cassettes, and books on herpes.
Call: (919) 361-8488 (9am-7pm EST).

FOUNDATION FOR THE PREVENTION OF VENEREAL DISEASE

This group can provide you with information on the prevention of sexually transmitted diseases. The foundation stresses the importance of responsible sexual relations and proper personal hygiene.
Write: American Foundation for the Prevention of Venereal Disease, 799 Broadway, Suite 638, New York, NY 10003 or **Call:** (212) 759-2069.

VENEREAL DISEASES

A free government booklet can be obtained on the symptoms, diagnosis, and treatment of diseases spread through sexual contact.
Write: NIH, The National Institute of Allergy and Infectious Diseases, Building 31, Room 7A32, Bethesda, MD 20205.

RAPE PREVENTION AND TREATMENT

A rape can be a very destructive event in the victim's life, and good professional help is needed to heal the wounds. Individuals specializing in this field should be sought out.

WOMEN AGAINST RAPE (W.A.R.)

A group working to prevent sexual abuse of women and/or children through education. W.A.R. works with preschool through college-age students, providing educational programs, films, and speakers. This organization counsels, provides shelter, and assists victims and their families. Publishes a brochure that offers tips for preventing child molestation and a coloring book *Child Watch* ($2.00) to help children distinguish good and bad touching.

Write: Women Against Rape (W.A.R), c/o Women Against Rape/Child Molestation, P. O. Box 346, Collingswood, NJ 08108 or **Call:** (609) 858-7800.

RAPE PREVENTION AND TREATMENT RESOURCES

A directory entitled *Sexual Assault and Child Sexual Abuse: A National Directory of Victim/Survivors Services and Prevention Programs* by Linda Webster is available from Orynx Press.

Write: Orynx Press, 2114 North Central at Encanto, Phoenix, AZ 85004-1483.

TALKING TO YOUR CHILD ABOUT SEXUAL ASSAULT

A booklet prepared by the King County Rape Relief volunteers and staff is an excellent parents' guide for talking to your child about sexual assault. It is entitled *He Told Me Not To Tell.*

Write: King County Sexual Assault Resource Center, 304 South Main, #200, Renton, WA 98055 or **Call:** (206) 226-RAPE; (206) 226-5062.

> *"Although the world is full of suffering, it is also full of the overcoming of it."*
>
> **Helen Keller**

TEENAGE SUICIDE We are all alarmed at the increased rate of teenage suicides. Programs are available for education and emergency intervention.

NATIONAL ADOLESCENT HOTLINE

A 24-hour hotline is maintained for runaway and suicide intervention.
Call: (800) 621-4000 (24 hours a day).

HIT HOME, NATIONAL YOUTH CRISIS HOTLINE

A youth-crisis hotline. Call to receive help for suicide, child abuse, depression, pregnancy, sexual abuse, and other crisis situations.
Write: Youth Development, Inc., P.O. Box 178408, San Diego, CA 92117-0910 or **Call:** (800) 448-4663 (24 hours a day).

AMERICAN ASSOCIATION OF SUICIDOLOGY

This national clearinghouse can send you free suicide-prevention pamphlets provided you send a stamped, self-addressed envelope. A.A.S. can also refer you to crisis lines and survivor support groups around the country. Information is available on setting up a school suicide-prevention program.
Write: American Association of Suicidology, 2459 South Ash Street, Denver, CO 80222 or **Call:** (303) 692-0985.

YOUTH SUICIDE NATIONAL CENTER

This national organization coordinates efforts to prevent youth suicides. Youth Suicide National Center can send you publications and a catalog ($2.00) if you will send a stamped, self-addressed envelope. Consultants are available to work with community and state educational systems in establishing suicide-prevention programs.
Write: Youth Suicide National Center, 204 E. Second Avenue, Suite 203, San Mateo, CA 94401 or **Call:** (415) 347-3961.

Captain Crimefighter's Drugbuster Program

The Sheriff's Office in Lake County, Florida has initiated a highly creative program to educate elementary children (K-5) about the dangers of drug use. It has created a superhero, Captain Crimefighter, who appears at schools for Captain Crimefighter's drugbuster programs. A special drugbuster hotline is provided for children to call the Sheriff's Office to communicate with Captain Crimefighter. This is an exemplary program for involving young people in the fight against drugs. It gives children the opportunity to know law-enforcement officers, not as policemen but as friends. If children write to Captain Crimefighter's address or call him, they will receive, at no cost, a letter from Captain Crimefighter along with a creed and a membership card that has Captain Crimefighter's picture on it. Please send a stamped, self-addressed envelope.

Write: Ron Hale and Earl Underwood, Captain Crimefighter Drugbuster Section, Lake County Sheriff's Office, 315 W. Main Street, Tavares, Florida 32778 or **Call:** (904) 343-7867.

3

ABUSED AND MISSING CHILDREN

CHILD ABUSE AND NEGLECT Nothing is more heartbreaking than an abused or neglected child. You may observe a child being abused and not know what to do. Programs exist to help both the child and parent. Also, advocacy groups exist that can assist a child in an underprivileged environment.

CHILD-ABUSE CLEARINGHOUSE

Information and publications are available from a national clearinghouse on child abuse. This clearinghouse can send you an excellent publication entitled *Child Sexual Abuse Prevention—Tips to Parents* (in English and Spanish). For definitions of child abuse, ways to report abuse, contacts at the local level, and reporting numbers for each state, a publication is available called *Child Abuse and Neglect: A Shared Community Concern.* Write for a free catalog of other publications.
Write: The Clearinghouse on Child Abuse and Neglect Information, P. O. Box 1182, Washington, DC 20013 or **Call:** (703) 821-2086.

24-HOUR CHILD-ABUSE HOTLINE

A 24-hour hotline exists where you can report suspected cases of child abuse. It can put you in touch with a number of services including treatment for abused and abandoned children.
Call: (800) 422-4453.

THE NATIONAL CENTER ON CHILD ABUSE AND NEGLECT

The NCCAN was established in 1974 to help professionals improve services to children and families in turmoil and to draw public attention to the problem of child maltreatment.
Write: National Center on Child Abuse and Neglect, 300 C Street, S.W., Washington, DC 20013 or **Call:** (202) 245-0814.

COMMITTEE FOR CHILDREN

This group can provide you with some excellent publications and videocassettes on child abuse. The publications include *Talking About Touching, A Personal Safety Curriculum* and *Talking About Touching with Preschoolers (for preschool teachers).* This training curricula are directed to preschool through eighth grade. A newly developed curriculum called Second Step, a violence prevention program designed to reduce impulsive and aggressive behavior in children and increase their level of social competency, is also available.
Write: Committee for Children, 172 20th Avenue, Seattle, WA 98122 or **Call:** (800) 634-4449; (206) 322-5050.

CHILD WELFARE LEAGUE OF AMERICA

A federation of 500 local agencies whose 140,000 staff members help over 2,000,000 abused, neglected, and deprived children each year.
Write: Child Welfare League of America, 440 First Street, Suite 310, N.W., Washington, DC 20001-2085 or **Call:** (202) 638-2952; CA (714) 599-4565.

NATIONAL COMMITTEE FOR PREVENTION OF CHILD ABUSE This organization is a national advocate for the development of social services to prevent child abuse. It can send you a free catalog of publications, and it can put you in touch with a local chapter in your state.
Write: National Committee for Prevention of Child Abuse, 332 S. Michigan Avenue, Suite 1600, Chicago, IL 60604-4357 or **Call:** (312) 663-3520.

AMERICAN ASSOCIATION FOR PROTECTING CHILDREN Agency which provides consultation and evaluation services to public/private sector-agencies, who in turn provide services to children and families. It conducts research and trains social workers. Publishes materials for professionals in the field regarding child abuse and neglect and the services involved in alleviating the problem. Division of American Humane founded in 1877.
Write: American Association for Protecting Children, 63 Inverness Drive East, Englewood, CO 80112-5117 or **Call:** (800) 227-5242; (303) 792-9900.

THE NATIONAL EXCHANGE CLUB FOUNDATION FOR THE PREVENTION OF CHILD ABUSE The foundation is a national project of the National Exchange Clubs, located in Toledo, Ohio. The success of the program is trained volunteer parent aides who enter the homes and lives of abusive families. The supportive relationship that develops between the volunteer parent aide and the family breaks the abuse cycle. The foundation currently has a network of 64 Centers in 30 states and Puerto Rico.
Write: The National Exchange Club Foundation for the Prevention of Child Abuse, 3050 Central Avenue, Toledo, Ohio 43606 or **Call:** (419) 535-3232.

LEGAL RESOURCES FOR CHILD-ABUSE CASES In child-abuse cases, it is advisable to consult attorneys who have specialized in this area. Below are some useful resources:

NATIONAL CENTER FOR PROSECUTION OF CHILD ABUSE Provides training and technical assistance to improve the investigation and prosecution of child abuse.
Write: National Center for Prosecution of Child Abuse, 1033 N. Fairfax Street, Suite 200, Alexandria, VA 22314 or **Call:** (703) 739-0321.

ABA CENTER ON CHILDREN AND THE LAW
Information clearinghouse that can provide attorneys with legal advice and training in the area of children's legal rights.
Write: Center on Children and the Law, American Bar Association, 1800 M Street, N.W., 2nd Floor, South Lobby, Washington, DC 20036 or **Call:** (202) 331-2250.

MENTAL HEALTH LAW PROJECT
This project protects mentally disabled children and adults from abuse and neglect in institutions and advocates comprehensive community-based services for the mentally disabled.
Write: Mental Health Law Project, 1101 15th Street, N.W., Suite 1212, Washington, DC 20005-5002 or **Call:** (202) 467-5730.

BURN-INJURY ABUSE TO CHILDREN
Sometimes it is difficult to determine whether a burn injury to a child is the result of abuse, neglect, or an accident. The National Burn Victim Foundation provides a forensic system to determine whether child burns are the result of abuse or and accident.
Write: National Burn Victim Foundation, 32-34 Scotland Road, Orange, NJ 07050 or **Call:** (201) 676-7700.

SELF-HELP GROUPS FOR THE ABUSED AND ABUSER One of the most effective means of breaking the child-abuse cycle in families is through counseling which involves others who have had to deal with this difficult problem.

PARENTS ANONYMOUS

An organization of parents who have either abused or fear they may harm their children either physically or emotionally, as well as others interested in the child-abuse problem. Its interest is in the prevention and treatment of child abuse. Parents Anonymous can put you in touch with one of over 1,200 chapters nationwide.
Write: Parents Anonymous, 6733 S. Sepulveda Boulevard, Suite 270, Los Angeles, CA 90045 or **Call:** (800) 421-0353; (213) 410-9732; (800) 352-0386 in California only.

PARENTS UNITED

A self-help group of individuals dealing with sexual-abuse problems. This group concerns itself primarily with incest. Provides support for families dealing with this problem, including counseling, coordination of community services, and working with the criminal justice system. Parents United has chapters nationwide, which include Daughters and Sons United and Adults Molested as Children United.
Write: Parents United, P.O. Box 952, San Jose, CA 95108 or **Call:** (408) 453-7611, Ex. 150.

"A happy childhood is one of the best gifts that parents have in their power to bestow."

R. Cholmondeley

MISSING AND EXPLOITED CHILDREN

A number of organizations exist that can help with missing and exploited children. Also, hotlines exist where information can be exchanged to assist in the location and recovery of missing children.

NATIONAL CENTER FOR MISSING AND EXPLOITED CHILDREN

This organization can provide free publications on missing and exploited children, including *Directory of Support Services and Resources for Missing and Exploited Children, Education and Prevention Guidelines,* and *Summary of Selected State Legislation—the Better Child-Protection Laws in the U.S.* A free booklet is available, entitled *Parental Kidnapping Handbook,* to help a parent who has had a child kidnapped.

Write: National Center for Missing and Exploited Children, 2101 Wilson Blvd., Suite 550, Arlington, VA 22201 or **Call:** (800) 843-5678 (24 hour); (703) 235-3900.

NATIONAL CENTER FOR MISSING YOUTH

Operation Lookout provides 24-hour intervention to legal custodians of missing children. It maintains a speakers' bureau and media lists. Can provide seminars for family-law attorneys on parental kidnapping. Hotline operators give immediate assistance to parents of missing children and anyone working to recover a missing child. It also responds to abducted children, runaways, and children separated from their parents.

Write: Operation Lookout, National Center for Missing Youth, P. O. Box 231, Mountlake Terrace, WA 98043 or **Call:** (800)782-SEEK; (206) 771-7335.

HOTLINE FOR MISSING AND EXPLOITED CHILDREN

A national hotline is maintained to exchange information that may lead to the location and recovery of a missing child. If you know of the location of a missing child, call this hotline.

Call: (800) 843-5678.

RECOVERING MISSING CHILDREN

A network of organizations and individuals exists throughout the United States and internationally which can assist in locating and recovering missing children.

CHILD FIND OF AMERICA, INC.

A national and international charitable organization that locates missing children and prevents child abduction through use of trained investigators and professional mediators and use of toll-free numbers. **Write:** Child Find, P. O. Box 277, New Paltz, NY 12561-9277 or **Call:** (800) I-AM-LOST (Missing Children); (800) A-WAY-OUT (Mediation Program).

EXPLOITED CHILDREN'S HELP ORGANIZATION

ECHO is a volunteer organization in Louisville, KY. It works on a national level with other nonprofit organizations and law-enforcement agencies. ECHO can send you a publication *What To Do If Your Child Is Missing*, which gives step-by-step instructions for parents who are trying to locate and recover a missing child. Also, a booklet can be provided on what to do if your child has been sexually abused. **Write:** ECHO, 720 W. Jefferson, Louisville, KY 40202 or **Call:** (502) 585-3246.

VANISHED CHILDREN'S ALLIANCE

An organization located in the San Francisco Bay area which offers location and recovery support to law-enforcement agencies and parents of missing children. Parents can receive technical assistance immediately following the missing incident by calling the Alliance headquarters. Support is provided to the family during the search process. It will help in the investigation. **Write:** Vanished Children's Alliance, 1407 Parkmoor Avenue, Suite200, San Jose, CA 95126 or **Call:** (800) 826-4743; (408) 971-4822.

NATIONAL CHILD SAFETY COUNCIL, MISSING CHILDREN DIVISION The NCSC operates a 24-hour toll-free hotline for sighting reports and information calls in regard to missing children. All calls are handled by trained professionals, and reports are made to the appropriate case-handling agency. A computerized nationwide database of missing children photographs and biographies is maintained on CompuServe Information Service in the Quick Pictures Forum.
Write: National Child Safety Council, Missing Children Division, P. O. Box 1368, Jackson, MI 49204-1368 or **Call:** (800) 222-1464: (517) 764-6070.

MISSING CHILDREN HELP CENTER
A national nonprofit organization which links missing children, their parents, and law enforcement. Helps families of children classified as criminally or parentally abducted, at risk/runaways, abandoned, unidentified bodies, and denied court-ordered visitations. Yearly mails 85,000 posters of missing children to law-enforcement agencies, truck stops, public schools, hospitals, news media, and civic organizations. Their Parents Taking Action Program encourages voluntary fingerprinting, crime watch and block-parent programs, absentee reporting systems, school psychologist and guidance counselor services, and criminal screening of day-care and baby-sitter professionals.
Write: Missing Children Help Center, 410 Ware Boulevard, Suite 400, Tampa, FL 33619 or **Call:** (813) 623-KIDS; (800) USA-KIDS.

CHILD KEYPPERS' INTERNATIONAL
This group sponsors *Exact-Ident Programs,* where children are fingerprinted and their teeth implanted with identifying materials. It has produced a record album entitled *Safety Key for Safety Wise Kids.*
Write: Child Keyppers' International, P. O. Box 6292, Lake Worth, FL 33466 or **Call:** (407) 586-6695.

NATIONAL MISSING CHILDREN'S LOCATE CENTER

A nonprofit organization [501(c)3] which assists parents in locating and recovering missing or abducted children. Promotes "Give'Em Back" a live call-in talk show which interviews parents, runaways, and experts in the field of missing and abducted children.

Write: National Missing Children's Locate Center, Inc., P. O. Box 1707, Gresham, OR 97030-0532 or **Call:** (503) 665-8544; (800) 443-2751 (out of state), Ext. 15; (800) 999-7846 (sightings only).

CHILDREN'S RIGHTS OF AMERICA, INC.

A nonprofit child-advocacy and youth-services organization. Provides direct support to help locate missing children including technical assistance to law enforcement and attorneys representing searching parents. It disseminates photographs of missing children to print and electronic media.

Write: Children's Rights of America, Inc., 655 Ulmerton Road, Suite 4A, Largo, FL 34641 or **Call:** (800) 874-1111 (Reporting Abuse); (800) 442-HOPE, (Teens-Crisis Line for under age 21); (813) 587-0122.

INTERNATIONAL CHILD ABDUCTION

The State Department can, through U.S. embassies and consulates overseas, render appropriate assistance to parents whose child has been abducted to a foreign country.

Write: The State Department, Bureau of Consular Affairs, CA/OCS/CCS, Room 4817, Washington, DC 20520 or **Call:** (202) 647-3666.

> *"Every place is safe to him who lives with justice."*
>
> Epictetus

PORNOGRAPHY AND OBSCENITY

Children are dependent on us to reduce their exposure to pornographic and obscene literature. Parents and teachers need to be constantly vigilant.

COALITION AGAINST PORNOGRAPHY

Provides victim referrals and information on resources available for victims of sexual abuse and sexual addiction. Educates the public about the harmful effects of pornography. Works on a national level to reduce sexual abuse by elimination of child pornography.
Write: National Coalition Against Pornography, 800 Compton Road, Suite 9224, Cincinnatti, OH 45231 or **Call:** (513) 521-6227.

CHILD-PORNOGRAPHY TIPLINE

A privately funded hotline in conjunction with the U.S. Customs Service is maintained to receive reports of child sexual exploitation.
Call: (800) 843-5678; TDD (800) 826-7653.

CHILD EXPLOITATION AND OBSCENITY

The Department of Justice has a unit staffed by senior attorneys who pursue and prosecute federal obscenity and child-pornography cases. It disseminates information on recent developments in obscenity and child-pornography law.
Write: U. S. Department of Justice, Child Exploitation and Obscenity Section, 10th and Constitution Avenue, N.W., Room 2216, Washington, DC 20530 or **Call:** (202) 514-5780.

NATIONAL COALITION FOR CHILDREN'S JUSTICE

Dedicated to improving protective services to the young and creating public awareness of social injustices to children.
Write: National Coalition for Children's Justice, 2119 Shelburne Road, Shelburne, VT 05482 or **Call:** (802) 985-8458.

TREATING EXPLOITED CHILDREN

Missing and exploited children are often severely damaged physically and emotionally. Professional help is needed and can be found at a number of centers around the United States.

ADAM WALSH CHILD RESOURCE CENTERS

These centers provide support and assistance to victimized children and their families. They assure that legal rights are protected and that public attention is given to the case when appropriate. Centers are located in Columbia, SC; West Palm Beach, FL; Rochester, NY; and Westminster, CA.

Call: SC(803) 254-2326; NY(716) 461-1000; (716) 244-8920; CA(714) 898-4802; FL(407) 820-9000.

VILLAGE OF CHILD HELP

A residential program which provides care and treatment for the abused child in a loving environment with a professional staff of many different specialists.

Write: Village of Child Help, P. O. Box 247, 14700 Manzantia Park Road, Beaumont, CA 92223 or **Call:** (714) 845-3155.

CHILDHELP, U.S.A.

This organization sponsors a number of activities geared toward preventing child abuse and helping abused children. Programs include residential treatment, foster care, and a national toll-free hotline for victims of abuse.

Write: Childhelp, U.S.A., Inc., 6463 Independence Avenue, Woodland Hills, CA 91367 or **Call:** (800) 4-A-CHILD.

> *"To sin by silence when they should protest makes cowards out of men."*
>
> Abraham Lincoln

4

CHILDREN'S HEALTH

GENERAL INFORMATION A number of clearinghouses and information centers exist that can point you in the right direction to find information on specific children's health-care problems. These people can also help you locate specialized treatment centers and support groups.

NATIONAL HEALTH INFORMATION CENTER

The ODPHP National Health Information Center can put you in touch with organizations that can answer your health-related questions. The National Health Information Center can provide you with names and addresses of appropriate organizations as well as refer your questions to organizations so that they can reply directly.
Write: ODPHP National Health Information Center, P.O. Box 1133, Washington, DC 20013-1133 or **Call:** (800) 336-4797.

CHILD-HEALTH INFORMATION

An institute at NIH can provide you the latest information on topics such as birth defects, developmental disabilities, sudden infant death syndrome, and infertility.
Write: National Institute of Child Health and Human Development, NIH, Department of Health and Human Services, 9000 Rockville Pike, Bethesda, MD 20892 or **Call:** (301) 496-5133.

DIRECTORY OF HEALTH SERVICES

You can obtain a directory from the Health Services Administration listing all its publications on various health subjects.
Write: Office of Public Affairs, Health Resources and Services Administration, Department of Health and Human Services, 5600 Fishers Lane, Room 1443, Rockville, MD 20857 or **Call:** (301) 443-2086.

NATIONAL CENTER FOR CLINICAL INFANT PROGRAMS NCCIP promotes the optimal health, mental health, and development of the nation's infants, toddlers, and families by training professionals, stimulating research, and educating policymakers. For a publications list, write the address below:
Write: National Center for Clinical Infant Programs, 2000 14th Street North, Suite 380, Arlington, VA 22201 or **Call:** (703) 528-4300.

ASSOCIATION FOR THE CARE OF CHILDREN'S HEALTH This organization, with 48 affiliates, focuses on the emotional needs of children and parents during a health-care experience. Membership is made up of parents and health-care professionals. Brochures (free or for a modest charge) are available for parents and children.
Write: Association for the Care of Children's Health (ACCH), 7910 Woodmont Avenue, Suite 300, Bethesda, MD 20814 or **Call:** (301) 654-6549.

MATERNAL AND CHILD HEALTH DATA BOOK The Children's Defense Fund has published a book that addresses the health of America's children ($12.95). It is a comprehensive examination of the complex factors affecting infant health, with extensive data for the nation and the states on birth outcome of teen pregnancies, infant mortalities, low-birthweight babies, prenatal care utilization, and federal and state benefits programs.
Write: Children's Defense Fund, 122 C Street, N.W., Suite 400, Washington DC 20001 or **Call:** (202) 628-8787.

AIDS This is rapidly becoming the number one health problem in the United States for children as well as adults. We and our children must become as well educated as possible to prevent its spread.

EDUCATING CHILDREN ABOUT AIDS

The Education Department has prepared a free booklet entitled *AIDS and the Education of Our Children: A Guide for Parents and Teachers.* It presents facts about AIDS, its transmission, and how teens are at risk. Methods of protection, guidelines for selecting educational materials, and sources for more information are included.
Write: Consumer Information Center, Dept. 509X, Pueblo, CO 81002.

AIDS HOTLINE

An AIDS hotline is maintained by the Department of Mental Health and Hygiene for adults and children. The hotline can refer you to testing sites and counseling.
Write: AIDS Hotline, 101 West Read Street, Suite 825, Baltimore, MD 21201 or **Call:** (800) 638-6252 (statewide toll free).

PHS AIDS HOTLINE

Three AIDS hotlines are maintained by the Public Health Service.
Call: (800) 342-AIDS (800) 342-2437 (24 hrs., 7 days a week).
(800) 243-7889 (Voice/TDD) (M-F, 10 a.m. - 10 p.m. E.S.T.).
(800) 344-7432 (Spanish) (7 days a wk. 8 a.m. - 2 a.m. E.S.T).

SUPPORT FOR CHILDREN WITH AIDS

A support organization that provides service, care, and preventive education for children and adults with AIDS. It provides housing for children with AIDS (e.g., Grandma's House in Washington, DC).
Write: Terrific Inc., Grandma's House, 1222 T Street N.W., Washington, DC 20009 or Call: (202) 462-8526.

HOW AIDS IS SPREAD

The government can send you a free booklet, *AIDS* (533X), which tells you how AIDS is spread, how to prevent it, and what to do if you think you've been infected.
Write: Consumer Information Center, Dept. 533X, Pueblo, CO 81009.

HOW TO DEAL WITH AIDS IN THE SCHOOL

The Department of Education has prepared a free booklet on facts about AIDS in our schools. It is entitled *AIDS and the Education of Our Children: A Guide for Parents and Teachers* (550X), and presents facts about AIDS, its transmission, and why adolescents are at risk. Methods of protection, guidelines for selecting AIDS educational materials, and local and national sources for additional information are listed.
Write: Consumer Information Center, Dept. 550X, Pueblo, Colorado 81009.

> *"Never mistake knowledge for wisdom. One helps make a living; the other helps you make a life."*
>
> Sandra Carey

ALLERGIES

ALLERGIES A variety of health and behavioral problems in young people is related to allergies. This is a specialized field where we are rapidly finding new answers.

AMERICAN ALLERGY ASSOCIATION

A group of patients and others interested in problems related to allergies. AAA disseminates information on food allergies, diet, environmental control, and other types of allergy advice. Please include a self-addressed, stamped envelope.
Write: American Allergy Association, P. O. Box 7273, Menlo Park, CA 94026.

AMERICAN ACADEMY OF ALLERGY AND IMMUNOLOGY

Allergies can have a profound effect on children's health and learning abilities. The American Academy of Allergy and Immunology can send you free literature on various allergies, such as asthma, hay fever, eczema, food allergies, and hives (send a self-addressed, stamped envelope). The Academy will also refer you to a specialist in your area.
Write: American Academy of Allergy and Immunology, 611 East Wells Street, Milwaukee, Wisconsin 53202 or **Call:** (800) 822-2762.

POLLEN ALLERGIES

Many young people suffer from pollen allergies and mistake them for the common cold. If symptoms are seasonal, you might suspect an allergic reaction to pollen. The National Institutes of Health has developed material which explains common pollen allergic reactions, treatments, and research ($1.00). Ask for the pamphlet, *Pollen Allergy.*
Write: Consumer Information Center, Dept. 126X, Pueblo, Colorado 81009.

ARTHRITIS Although arthritis is thought of as primarily an adult disease, it also takes its toll among our young people.

ARTHRITIS FOUNDATION

An organization concerned with rheumatic diseases. The Arthritis Foundation is dedicated to the discovery of the cause of these diseases and better methods for their treatment and prevention. Literature is available.

Write: Arthritis Foundation, 2307 Chapline Street, Wheeling, WV 26003 or **Call:** WV (800) 479-5044; (304) 232-5810.

ASTHMA Children who suffer from asthmatic attacks need special attention. It is good to have them checked by a specialist who treats asthmatics. The agencies listed below can help you find such specialists:

ASTHMA AND ALLERGY FOUNDATION OF AMERICA An agency that offers information and a referral service. The foundation can provide practical help nationwide to asthma and allergy sufferers. It provides medical and social rehabilitation for chronic asthmatics. and operates an allergy outpatient clinic for all age groups with written referrals. Publications are available, e.g., *What is Asthma? What is Allergy?*

Write: Asthma and Allergy Foundation of America, 1125 15th Street, N.W., Suite 502, Washington, DC 20005 or **Call:** (800) 7-ASTHMA; (202) 466-7643.

"Courage is fear that has said its prayers."

Anonymous

BLOOD DISEASES It is important that blood diseases be diagnosed promptly and properly.

CHILDREN'S BLOOD FOUNDATION

The oldest and largest organization dedicated to care, research, and medical training for children with blood diseases and cancers. The Children's Blood Foundation exists to support the Division of Pediatric Hematology Oncology at The New York Hospital-Cornell Medical Center. Designated by the American Board of Pediatrics as the premier hematology/oncology facility in the United States. Children receive comprehensive care for thalassemia, hemophilia, leukemia, AIDS, sickle cell anemia, ITP, chronic anemias, retinoblastoma – virtually every blood disease that affects children.
Write: Children's Blood Foundation, Inc., 424 E. 62nd Street, Room 1045, New York, NY 10021 or **Call:** (212) 644-5790.

COOLEY'S ANEMIA FOUNDATION

Cooley's anemia is a blood disease that requires frequent transfusions to keep its victims alive. This organization provides life-preserving medication, infusion pumps, batteries, family support, professional and public education, and funds research on thalassemia, a fatal genetic blood disorder which strikes children.
Write: Cooley's Anemia Foundation, 105 E. 22nd Street, Suite 911, New York, NY 10010 or **Call:** (800) 522-7222; NY (800) 221-3571; (212) 598-0911.

NATIONAL HEMOPHILIA FOUNDATION

This organization provides support and information for individuals dealing with hemophilia.
Write: National Hemophilia Foundation, 110 Green Street, Room 303, New York, NY 10012 or **Call:** (212) 219-8180.

SICKLE CELL DISEASE

This is a common blood disorder. The National Association for Sickle Cell Disease can answer your questions about sickle cell disease as it relates to young people. It distributes fact sheets about sickle cell and pregnancy, and how the disease is passed from parent to child.
Write: National Association for Sickle Cell Disease, 3345 Wilshire Boulevard, Suite 1106, Los Angeles, CA 90010-1880 or **Call:** (800) 421-8453.

CANCER Some of the bravest people in the world are children with cancer. Much progress has been made in the treatment of cancers, and numerous people are standing by to help children suffering from this disease.

CANCER INFORMATION SERVICE

This toll-free hotline can provide information on prevention, diagnosis, treatment, and confidential counseling.
Write: Cancer Information Service, National Cancer Institute, Building 31, Room 10A24, 9000 Rockville Pike, Bethesda, MD 20892 or **Call:** (800) 4 – CANCER; (800) 422-6237.

AMERICAN CANCER SOCIETY

The American Cancer Society's work with children and cancer includes a number of free booklets and videotapes for children in treatment, siblings and parents of a child in treatment, and children who have a parent in cancer treatment. Titles include *What Happened to You Happened to Me*; *It Helps to Have Friends (When Mom or Dad Have Cancer)*; *Mister Rogers Talks about Childhood Cancer;* and *Back to School–A Handbook for the Parents of Children with Cancer.* Contact your local unit of the American Cancer Society listed in your phone book for more information on booklets or programs for children in your area.
Write: American Cancer Society, 1599 Clifton Road, N.E., Atlanta, GA 30329 or **Call:** (800) ACS-2345; (404) 320-3333.

LEUKEMIA SOCIETY OF AMERICA

This society can provide patients and families of children with leukemia information, phone counseling, and free literature. Financial aid is also available for qualified outpatients being treated for leukemia, lymphomas, and multiple myeloma and Hodgkins disease.
Write: Leukemia Society of America, 2900 Eisenhower Avenue, Suite 419, Alexandria, VA 22314 or **Call:** (703) 960-1100 (may call collect).

CANDLELIGHTERS CHILDHOOD CANCER FOUNDATION

An international organization of parents whose children/adolescents have or have had cancer. Four hundred self-help groups throughout the country. Quarterly and youth newsletters, bibliography, and other educational materials available.
Write: Candlelighters Childhood Cancer Foundation, 1312 18th Street, N.W., #200, Washington, DC 20036 or **Call:** (202) 659-5136; (800) 366-2223.

CORPORATE ANGEL NETWORK (CAN)

The Corporate Angel Network is a nationwide program designed to give cancer patients the use of available seats on corporate aircraft to get to or from recognized treatment. Travel is not guaranteed, so backup reservations must be made. There is no cost to the patient, nor are there any financial-need criteria. Requests for transportation should be made when a definite date for an appointment or for discharge has been arranged.
Write: CAN, Building One, Westchester County Airport, White Plains, NY 10604 or **Call:** (914) 328-1313.

> *"Kindness is the sunshine in which virtue grows."*
>
> **R. B. Ingersoll**

CYSTIC FIBROSIS This congenital disease of children is characterized by a malfunctioning of the pancreas and frequent respiratory infections.

CYSTIC FIBROSIS FOUNDATION

This foundation sponsors over 120 care centers for cystic fibrosis victims nationally. Can refer you to facilities near you for this inherited disease among children and young adults. This foundation provides information to the public and training to health professionals and therapists. The Cystic Fibrosis Foundation provides a pharmacy service, which can result in considerable savings to CF patients and their families.
Write: Cystic Fibrosis Foundation, 6931 Arlington Road, #200, Bethesda, MD 20814 or **Call:** (800) FIGHT CF; (301) 951-4422.

DIABETES This disease can sometimes be difficult to diagnose. It's important that it be diagnosed and treated early in children as well as adults.

AMERICAN DIABETES ASSOCIATION

Promotes the free exchange of knowledge about diabetes by educating the public in the early detection of this disorder. Educational material is available to give diabetics a better understanding of their disease.
Write: American Diabetes Association, 505 8th Avenue, New York, NY 10018 or **Call:** (212) 947-9707.

JOSLIN DIABETES CENTER

This organization sponsors two camps for diabetic children, maintains an inpatient diabetes treatment unit to instruct patients of all ages in the proper management of their disease, runs support groups for parents and children, and publishes a series of books on diabetes, including several specifically for children.
Write: Joslin Diabetes Center, One Joslin Place, Boston, MA 02215 or **Call:** (617) 732-2440.

<u>DIABETES RESEARCH INSTITUTE FOUNDATION</u>

A coalition of private citizens, international research scientists, and clinicians dedicated to improving the quality of life for people afflicted with diabetes. Recognized worldwide for excellence in basic and clinical research, specialized patient care, and comprehensive educational programs for health professionals, patients, and their families, the institute's mission is to find a permanent cure for more than 12 million children and adults living with diabetes.

Write: Diabetes Research Institute Foundation, 8600 N.W. 53rd Terrace, Suite 202, Miami, FL 33166 or **Call:** (800) 321-3437; (305) 477-3437.

DIGESTIVE DISORDERS A variety of maladies can occur in the digestive tract of young people as well as adults. Some of these are related to dietary habits and food allergies.

<u>CROHN'S & COLITIS FOUNDATION OF AMERICA</u>

Supports research and education programs, medical symposia, and self-help groups to help the estimated 2 million Americans afflicted with inflammatory bowel disease.

Write: Crohn's & Colitis Foundation of America, 444 Park Avenue, South, 11th floor, New York, NY10016 or **Call:** (800) 343-3637; NY (212) 685-3440.

"It is not easy taking my problems one at a time when they refuse to get in line."

Ashleigh Brilliant

GLUTEN INTOLERANCE GROUP

Some children have an inherited disorder that is expressed as a gluten-related destruction of the small intestine. This organization offers children's services and group and individual counseling for those suffering from this disorder. It also publishes a gluten-free diet book, cookbook, and fact sheets.

Write: Gluten Intolerance Group of North America, P. O. Box 23053, Seattle, WA 98102-0353 or **Call:** (206) 325-6980.

NATIONAL REGISTRY FOR MPS/ML DISORDERS

An organization of family members with children suffering from MPS (mucopolysaccharidosis) or ML (mucolipidosis), which involves the abnormal storage of carbohydrates in children. It can provide a referral service linking families to support groups or other helpful agencies.

Write: March of Dimes National Registry for MPS/ML Disorders, c/o Community Services Dept., One N. Dearborn, Suite 1008, Chicago, IL 60602 or **Call:** (312) 407-4007.

HEART DISORDERS

This vital organ is generally taken for granted until it malfunctions. A healthy heart has added importance in a young person.

AMERICAN HEART ASSOCIATION

This organization can send you educational pamphlets on diet and exercise for children and adults and their effects on health. AHA also has pamphlets on different types of heart disease and stroke. Single copies are free. There is a charge for bulk quantities.

Write: National Center of the American Heart Association, 7320 Greenville Avenue., Dallas, TX 75231 or **Call:** (214) 706-1179.

IMMUNIZATION

IMMUNIZATION Disease prevention through immunization is an important part of child health care. It is important that you stay informed as to what shots your child may need and their possible side effects.

GUIDE TO CHILDHOOD IMMUNIZATION

A $1.25 booklet *Parent's Guide to Childhood Immunization* (140X) tells you how vaccines protect your child from eight serious diseases and possible side effects to watch for. Includes immunization schedules.
Write: Consumer Information Center, Dept. 140X, Pueblo, CO 81009.

NATIONAL VACCINE INFORMATION CENTER

A nonprofit, educational organization of parents and professionals concerned abut childhood diseases and the safety and effectiveness of all vaccines, especially the DPT vaccine. This organization can refer parents to support services and assist in reporting adverse reactions related to vaccines.
Write: National Vaccine Information Center, 128 Branch Road, Vienna, VA 22180 or **Call:** (703) 938-3783.

> *"Fewer than 60 percent of children under age 4 are immunized against basic diseases such as measles and mumps."*
>
> **Washington Post, 1989**

INJURIES Children often sustain tragic injuries. It is important that they receive prompt and adequate treatment to insure full recovery.

BRAIN-INJURED CHILDREN

A self-help group of parents of brain-injured children and young adults exists which can provide you with support and information. Can provide counseling, educational material, and assistance to families and injured individuals.
Write: A Chance to Grow, 5034 Oliver Avenue, N., Minneapolis, MN 55430 or **Call:** (612) 521-2266.

EFFECTS OF HEAD INJURIES ON CHILDREN

The National Head Injury Foundation can send you a number of publications relative to the effects of head injuries on children. Included are *Effects of Major and Minor Head Injury in Children* and *Minor Head Injury in Children–Out of Sight But Not Out of Mind.*
Write: The National Head Injury Foundation, 1140 Connecticut Avenue, N.W., Suite 812, Washington, DC 20036 or **Call:** Family Helpline (800) 444-6443; (202) 296-6443.

THE NATIONAL HEAD INJURY FOUNDATION

The National Head Injury Foundation is dedicated to improving the quality of life for individuals with head injury and their families through education, support, advocacy, and prevention activities. It has 44 state chapters and more than 350 support groups available nationwide. NHIF is a clearinghouse for information and resources related to head injury. Write for a free *Catalogue of Educational Materials.*
Write: The National Head Injury Foundation, 1140 Connecticut Avenue, N.W., Suite 812, Washington, DC 20036 or **Call:** (202) 296-NHIF; (800) 444-NHIF (Family Helpline).

NATIONAL SPINAL CORD INJURY ASSOCIATION

Founded by Paralyzed Veterans of America. Provides information, referrals, and support; through local chapters nationwide, provides prevention programs and services.
Write: National Spinal Cord Injury Association, 600 West Cummings Park, Suite 2000, Woburn, MA 01801 or **Call:** (800) 962-9629.

KIDNEY DISORDERS If this organ malfunctions, toxicity occurs rapidly in the body. Infections of the kidney must be treated very seriously.

NATIONAL KIDNEY FOUNDATION

Provides patient/community service, public/professional education, and research support for treatment, prevention, and cure of kidney and urologic disease.
Write: National Kidney Foundation, 30 East 33rd Street, New York, NY 10016 or **Call:** (800) 622-9010; (212) 889-2210.

AMERICAN KIDNEY FUND

This organization can provide direct financial assistance to needy kidney-disease victims.The American Kidney Fund has brochures and can make available slide/tape presentations.
Write: American Kidney Fund, 6110 Executive Boulevard, Suite 1010, Rockville, MD 20852 or **Call:** (800) 638-8299.

"A child can ask a thousand questions that the wisest man cannot answer."

Jacob Abbott

LIVER DISORDERS

This detoxifying organ must function properly for proper health. In small infants this is particularly critical.

CHILD LIVER FOUNDATION

For parents and friends of children with liver disorders and other interested people. Can provide information and advice on treatment centers.
Write: Children's Liver Foundation, 14245 Ventura Blvd., Suite 201, Sherman Oaks, CA 91423 or **Call:** (818) 906-3021.

AMERICAN LIVER FOUNDATION

A national voluntary organization dedicated to fighting all liver diseases, in both children and adults, through research, education, and patient self-help groups.
Write: American Liver Foundation, 1425 Pompton Avenue, Suite 1-3, Cedar Grove, NJ 07009 or **Call:** (201) 256-2550.

LUNG DISORDERS

Breathing oxygen is essential to life. There are many lung disorders that make breathing more difficult for a child. Children in households with smokers may also suffer ill effects, such as cancer of the lung.

AMERICAN LUNG ASSOCIATION

Information for all who are interested in the prevention and control of lung disease.
Write: American Lung Association, 1740 Broadway, New York, NY 10019 or **Call:** (212) 315-8700.

LUNG LINE

This service is sponsored by the National Jewish Center for Immunology and Respiratory Medicine. Trained nurses will answer your questions about the detection and care of such diseases as asthma, emphysema, chronic bronchitis, tuberculosis, juvenile rheumatoid arthritis, and food and other allergies.
Write: Lung Line, 1400 Jackson Street, Denver, CO 80206 or **Call:** (800) 222-LUNG or (303) 355-LUNG in Denver metropolitan area.

NEUROLOGICAL DISEASES Children suffer from a number of disabling neurological diseases. Early diagnosis and treatment is imperative.

MUSCULAR DYSTROPHY ASSOCIATION

MDA supports scientific investigators seeking the causes of and effective treatments for muscular dystrophy and related neuromuscular disorders. It sponsors a broad program of selected patient and community services in addition to research. At the present time this association sponsors a network of some 230 clinics coast-to-coast to provide diagnostic services and therapeutic rehabilitative follow-up as well as genetic and social service counseling and emotional support services to those with neuromuscular disorders and their families.
Write: Muscular Dystrophy Association, Patient and Community Services Department, 3561 East Sunrise Drive, Tuscon, AZ 85718 or **Call:** (800) 223-6666; (602) 529-2000.

NATIONAL MULTIPLE SCLEROSIS SOCIETY

This group can provide services and aid for persons having MS. It offers on-line computer searches for biomedical databases.
Write: National Multiple Sclerosis Society, 205 E. 42nd Street, New York, NY 10017 or **Call:** (800) 624-8236; (212) 986-3240; 24-hour tape message with information about resources.

EPILEPSY FOUNDATION OF AMERICA

National voluntary health agency that serves as the "focal point for the fight against epilepsy in the U.S." It can send you educational material.
Write: Epilepsy Foundation of America, 4351 Garden City Drive, Landover, MD 20785 or **Call:** (800) 332-1000; (301) 459-3700.

> *"Compassion must lead to action."*
>
> Barbara Patton

UNITED CEREBRAL PALSY ASSOCIATION

This organization can tell you about steps to prevent this disability. UCPA also has information on how to manage the disability for those who have it. Free booklets are available, entitled *Do's and Don'ts for Prospective Mothers* and *Cerebral Palsy: Facts and Figures*.
Write: United Cerebral Palsy Association, 7 Penn Plaza, Suite 804, New York, NY 10001 or **Call:** (800) USA-1UCP; (212) 268-6655.

AMERICAN NARCOLEPSY ASSOCIATION (ANA)

Is your child sleepy every day? This could be a sign of a serious disease – narcolepsy. This agency helps with free information and referrals for diagnosis and treatment. Nationwide coverage.
Write: American Narcolepsy Association, P.0. Box 26230, San Francisco, CA 94126 or **Call:** (415) 788-4793.

AMERICAN PARALYSIS ASSOCIATION

Dedicated to the support of research for paralysis caused by spinal cord injury and other central nervous system disorders. The APA Spinal Cord Injury Hotline provides referral service for the spinal cord injured, their families, and assistance for professionals working in the field who need assistance.
Write: American Paralysis Association, 500 Morris Avenue, Springfield, NJ 07081 or **Call:** (800) 526-3456 Hotline; NJ (800) 225-0292.

ORTON DYSLEXIA SOCIETY

Dyslexia is a neurological disorder that impairs reading. If undetected in children, it can create major learning problems. For $3.00 this organization will send you an information package on detecting and dealing with dyslexia.
Write: The Orton Dyslexia Society, Chester Building, Suite 382, 8600 LaSalle Road, Baltimore, MD 21204-6020 or **Call:** (800) 222-2123; (800) ABCD-123; (301) 296-0232.

ORGAN TRANSPLANTS A child's life sometimes hangs on the rapid procurement and transplantation of a vital organ. Organizations exist which can assist in matching patients needs with donated organs.

CHILDREN'S TRANSPLANT ASSOCIATION

This organization provides support to families of children needing organ transplants. The Children's Transplant Association will purchase airline tickets for evaluations and offer emergency air transportation at the time transplants are made. In addition, it helps with lodging, food, transportation, and other necessities. CTA will intervene on your behalf against private insurance companies as well as state medicaid. It owns its own residence facilities at two major transplant centers and is building more.

Write: Children's Transplant Association, P. O. Box 53699, Dallas, TX 75253 or **Call:** (214) 287-8484.

UNITED NETWORK FOR ORGAN SHARING

Serves as a clearinghouse for organs used in U.S. transplant operations. Operates the Organ Center, which matches patients in need of transplants with donated organs and arranges for transport of the organs to needed locations.

Write: United Network for Organ Sharing, 1100 Boulders Parkway, Richmond, VA 23225 or **Call:** (804) 330-8500.

ORGAN DONORS

The Living Bank is the national organ and tissue donor registry, providing information to those who are interested in donating organs or tissue at the time of death.

Write: Organ Donors, P.O. Box 6725, Houston, TX 77265 or **Call:** (800) 528-2971; (713) 961-9431.

RARE DISORDERS Although a number of maladies that children suffer are rare, this doesn't make them any less difficult for those who suffer with them.

NATIONAL ORGANIZATION FOR RARE DISORDERS

This organization is dedicated to preventing, controlling, and curing rare disabilities and to helping people afflicted by these devastating illnesses.
Write: National Organization for Rare Disorders, P.O. Box 8923, New Fairfield, Connecticut 06812-1783 or **Call:** (800) 999-6673.

ORGANIZATION FOR ALBINISM & HYPOPIGMENTATION

This group provides information and emotional support for individuals and families with albinism, promotes public and professional education about albinism, and encourages research and research funding that will lead to improved diagnosis and treatment. Can send you pamphlets on these subjects.
Write: National Organization for Albinism and Hypopigmentation, 1500 Locust Street, Suite 1816, Philadelphia, PA 19102 or **Call:** (215) 545-2322; (800) 473-2310.

NATIONAL ATAXIA FOUNDATION

Ataxia is similar to multiple sclerosis; however, MS is not inherited and has a different origin. This organization can provide information and services to ataxia victims and their families.
Write: National Ataxia Foundation, 750 Twelve Oaks Center, 15500 Wayzata Boulevard, Wayzata, MN 55391 or **Call:** (612) 473-7666.

SCLERODERMA FEDERATION

Scleroderma is a chronic disease which can be either localized or systemic, and is caused by an excess of collagen in body tissues. This organization provides outreach, educational materials, a helpline, and access to local support groups.
Write: Scleroderma Federation, 1725 York Avenue, # 29F, New York, NY 10128 or **Call:** (212) 427-7040.

CORNELIA DE LANGE SYNDROME FOUNDATION

Cornelia De Lange syndrome is a rare birth defect of unknown cause that results in low-birthweight babies who develop at a less than normal rate. This organization works toward early diagnosis of this problem and can provide members with medical updates on research. **Write:** Cornelia De Lange Syndrome Foundation, c/o Julie Mairano, 60 Dyer Avenue, Collinsville, CT 06022 or **Call:** (800) 223-8355; (203) 693-0159.

NATIONAL HYDROCEPHALUS FOUNDATION

Hydrocephalus is caused by a buildup of fluid in the brain cavity. This organization aims to resolve specific problems that parents of children with hydrocephalus encounter. It will send you literature on this subject.
Write: National Hydrocephalus Foundation, 22427 S. River Road, Joliet, IL 60436 or **Call:** (815) 467-6548 (after 4:00 pm). Moving to new office in Wrigley Bldg. in Chicago soon (check for new number).

RETT SYNDROME ASSOCIATION

Rett syndrome strikes only females who appear normal until seven to 18 months of age, when autisticlike withdrawal sets in. This organization is concerned with promoting research on this disorder. This association can send you a brochure, *What Is Rett Syndrome?* It is also involved with parent support and with the dissemination of accurate and objective information.
Write: International Rett Syndrome Association, 8511 Rose Marie Drive, Ft. Washington, MD 20744 or **Call:** (301) 248-7031.

NATIONAL TAY-SACHS ASSOCIATION

Tay-Sachs is a degenerative disease occurring in infants and children. This organization sponsors massive screening programs to detect the disease. It can provide you with educational materials on this disorder.
Write: National Tay-Sachs and Allied Diseases Association, 2001 Beacon Street, Brookline, MA 02146 or **Call:** (617) 277-4463.

TOURETTE SYNDROME ASSOCIATION

This disorder is characterized by ticlike muscular movements and involuntary utterances. This organization works to assist individuals and families dealing with this problem. It maintains a library and a list of doctors familiar with this disorder.

Write: Tourette Syndrome Association, 42-40 Bell Boulevard, Bayside, NY 11361 or **Call:** (800) 237-0717: (718) 224-2999.

TUBEROUS SCLEROSIS (NTSA)

TS is a rare genetic disorder (cause and cure unknown) that may affect a number of organs and result in mental retardation. The National Tuberous Sclerosis Association, Inc., can refer you to clinics and support groups and send you literature on this disease.

Write: National Tuberous Sclerosis Association, Inc., 8000 Corporate Drive, Suite 120, Landover, MD 20785 or **Call:** (800) 225-6872; (301) 459-9888.

REYE'S SYNDROME

This infant disease is not fully understood. Some evidence links it to the treatment of flu or chicken pox.

NATIONAL REYE'S SYNDROME FOUNDATION

This group informs and educates the public, supports research, and provides services to victims of Reye's Syndrome, a fatal disease whose cause is unknown. Although a major cause of death in children ages 1–10. Reye's does affect adults and is often misdiagnosed.This organization will respond to your questions about Reye's Syndrome. It can send you literature and put you in touch with local organizations that can help.

Write: National Reye's Syndrome Foundation, P. O. Box 829, 426 North Lewis, Bryan, Ohio 43506 or **Call:** (800) 233-7393; Ohio (800) 231-7393.

SCOLIOSIS This disorder involves a curvature of the spine that can eventually become crippling. It is imperative that scoliosis be detected and treated early in children.

SCOLIOSIS ASSOCIATION

An association that encourages spinal screening programs in schools throughout the U.S. for the detection of scoliosis (a lateral or sideward curvature of the spine). The Scoliosis Association has a bibliography of scoliosis citations, literature, and posters. It establishes self-help group chapters for patients and families.
Write: Scoliosis Association, P. O. Box 51353, Raleigh, NC 27609-1353 or **Call:** (919) 846-2639.

SKIN DISORDERS Skin problems can cause young people major difficulties and can become debilitating in the case of severe cystic acne. Overexposure to the sun or tanning lights can also increase the odds of a young person's developing skin cancer.

SKIN CANCER FOUNDATION

This group can send you the latest information on sunscreen products which will prevent skin cancers. Also it has booklets, posters, and charts on the prevention of skin cancer.
Write: Skin Cancer Foundation, 245 Fifth Avenue, Suite 2402, New York, NY 10016 or **Call:** (212) 725-5176.

TANNING AND SKIN CANCER

Excessive tanning can lead to skin cancer. A free pamphlet *"Healthy Tan" – A Fast-Fading Myth* (523X) is available. It presents symptoms of skin cancer and the benefits of protecting the skin.
Write: Consumer Information Center, Dept. 523X, Pueblo, CO 81009.

NATIONAL NEUROFIBROMATOSIS FOUNDATION

Stimulates and supports research on NF (neurofibromatosis), educates patients, families, health-care professionals about NF, and works to establish diagnostic standards and protocols for NF.
Write: National Neurofibromatosis Foundation, 141 5th Avenue, Suite 7S, New York, NY 10010 or **Call:** (800) 323-7938; NY (212) 460-8980.

SPECIAL PROBLEMS OF ADOLESCENT

A major concern of adolescents is early or late physical development. The hormonal changes that initiate puberty usually begin at about the age 10 or 11 in girls and about 12 or 13 in boys. A wide variation exists in adolescent growth patterns, and most of these can be considered normal according to the American Medical Association.

A girl whose mother started her periods comparatively late is likely to begin menstruation late herself. A boy's development is likely to follow the same pattern as his father's.

Parents can ease the pain of children who are not developing as fast as their peers by assuring them that the "differences" are only temporary.

SPINA BIFIDA This is a common birth defect, which must receive immediate attention to prevent paralysis.

SPINA BIFIDA ASSOCIATION OF AMERICA

Spina bifida, "open spine," is the leading disabler of newborns in America and results in muscle weakness and paralysis. This organization can provide you information on its treatment.
Write: Spina Bifida Association of America, 1700 Rockville Pike, Suite 250, Rockville, MD 20852 or **Call:** (800) 621-3141; (301) 770-7222.

SUDDEN INFANT DEATH Few things can be more devastating than the sudden, unexpected death of an infant. We are rapidly gaining a better understanding of the causes of this puzzling syndrome.

SIDS ALLIANCE

The SIDS Alliance operates a national referral program to respond to questions and concerns about SIDS. This organization can identify local resources available to SIDS families, interested health professionals, and the public. Available are booklets entitled *Facts About SIDS, How Shall We Tell The Children,* and *The Subsequent Children,* as well as other materials.
Write: SIDS Alliance, 10500 Little Patuxent Parkway, Suite 420, Columbia, MD 21044 or **Call:** (800) 221-7437; (301) 964-8000.

NATIONAL SUDDEN INFANT DEATH SYNDROME CLEARINGHOUSE

A clearinghouse that can supply you fact sheets, bibliographies, directories, booklets, and *Information Exchange,* which is a national forum for sharing SIDS-related news. It can send you a catalog listing its publications.
Write: National Sudden Infant Death Syndrome Clearinghouse, 8201 Greensboro Drive, Suite 600, McLean, VA 22102 or **Call:** (703) 821-8955.

> *"So softly death succeeded life in her. She did but dream of Heaven and she was there."*
>
> John Dryden

WISH FULFILLMENT FOR CHILDREN WITH LIFE-THREATENING ILLNESSES

Fortunately, we live in a society with a heart. A number of organizations and volunteers exist that will help enrich the life of a terminally or chronically ill child.

NATIONAL ALLIANCE OF WISH GRANTING ORGANIZATIONS (NAGO) An organization of wish-granting organizations whose members adhere to a set of ethical and public relations standards. Call if you have questions about a wish-granting organization. A directory is available. It also has a speakers' bureau.
Write: National Alliance of Wish Granting Organizations, 3200 Wayne, Suite 106, Kansas City, MO 64109 or **Call:** (800) 666-WISH.

THE BRASS RING SOCIETY

A society which seeks to fulfill the dreams of children with life-threatening illnesses. It has a variety of programs, including granting wishes, providing books, equipment, and other hospital needs and services. National in scope.
Write: The Brass Ring Society, 314 Main Street, Ottawa, KS 66067 or **Call:** (800) 666-WISH; (913) 242-1666.

THE GRANT-A-WISH FOUNDATION

Has a variety of programs designed to ease the burden of long hospital stays and painful treatment programs for children. It grants wishes to individual children and provides seashore and mountain retreats and in-hospital entertainment programs. Also manages the Children's House at Johns Hopkins.
Write: The Grant-A-Wish Foundation, P. O. Box 21211, Baltimore, MD 21228 or **Call:** (301) 242-1549; (800) 933-5470.

HIGH HOPES FOUNDATION OF NEW HAMPSHIRE

Volunteer organization dedicated to granting wishes of seriously ill New Hampshire children from birth to 18 years old.
Write: High Hopes Foundation of New Hampshire, P.O. Box 172, North Salem, New Hampshire 03073 or **Call:** (603) 898-5333.

DREAM FACTORY

Organization seeking to "bring smiles to the faces of seriously ill children" by granting their greatest wish. Sponsors an annual summer camp for children.
Write: Dream Factory, P. O. Box 3942, Louisville, KY 40201-3942 or **Call:** (800) 456-7556.

MAKE-A-WISH FOUNDATION OF AMERICA

Organization that grants wishes to kids ages 2 1/2 to 18 suffering from life-threatening illnesses which create the probability that children will not survive beyond their 18th birthday.
Write: Make-A-Wish Foundation of America, 2600 N. Central Avenue, Suite 936, Phoenix, AZ 85004 or **Call:** (602) 240-6600.

STARLIGHT FOUNDATION

This group will help arrange and finance special trips or other wishes of chronically, critically, and terminally ill children, 4 to 18 years of age.
Write: Starlight Foundation, 10920 Wilshire Blvd., Suite 1640, Los Angeles, CA 90024 or **Call:** (800) 274-7827; (213) 208-5885.

<u>THE SUNSHINE FOUNDATION</u> This organization grants dreams and wishes of terminally and chronically ill children whose parents are under financial strain, due to the child's illness.
Write: Sunshine Foundation, 4010 Levick Street, Philadelphia, PA 19135 or **Call:** (800) 767-1976; (215) 335-2622.

OPERATION LIFTOFF

Established to fulfill the wishes of terminally ill children.
Write: Operation Liftoff, 1171 Kings Avenue, Ben Salem, PA 19020 or **Call:** (215) 639-1586; Kansas (816) 454-5557; Louisiana (504) 431-7451; Maine (207) 848-3157; Missouri (314) 867-5961; Ohio (614) 245-9535; Wisconsin (715) 684-3181.

SPECIAL LOVE, INC.

A nonprofit organization providing enriching programs for children with cancer. They sponsor Camp Fantastic.
Write: Camp Fantastic, P. O. Box 3243, Winchester, VA 22601 or **Call:** (703) 667-3774.

A WISH WITH WINGS

Raises funds to grant the wishes of children ages 3-16 who suffer from life-threatening illnesses. A Wish With Wings can provide toys, trips, or introductions to celebrities and other "greatest wishes."
Write: A Wish With Wings, P. O. Box 3457, Arlington, TX 76010 or **Call:** (817) 469-9474; (708) 246-2723.

CHILDREN'S WISH FOUNDATION INTERNATIONAL

A foundation that fills the wishes of terminally ill children under 18. It has an international program.
Write: Children's Wish Foundation International, 8215 Roswell Road, Bldg. 200, Suite 100, Atlanta, GA 30350 or **Call:** (800) 323-9474.

DREAMS COME TRUE

An organization that fulfills the dreams of children with life-threatening illnesses who are referred by their physicians, are under the age of 18 years, and are treated in the Jacksonville, Florida, area.
Write: Dreams Come True, 8184 Baymeadows Way West, Jacksonville, FL 32256 or **Call:** (904) 733-1010.

SUPPORT FOR ILL CHILDREN AND THEIR FAMILIES

Some extra attention is available for ill children through various support organizations.

FAMOUS FONE FRIENDS

If a sick child's doctor or nurse contacts FFF, they can arrange for a well-known actor, athlete, or other celebrity to call the child for a friendly chat.

Write: Famous Fone Friends, 9101 Sawyer Street, Los Angeles, CA 90035 or **Call:** (213) 204-5683.

LAUGHTER THERAPY

These people can supply tapes of old *Candid Camera* movies to patients. Maintains a library of 50 topics.

Write: Laughter Therapy, P. O. Box 827, Monterey, CA 93940 or **Call:** (408) 625-3788.

THE HOLIDAY PROJECT

At Christmas, Hanukkah, and other holidays, Holiday Project volunteers visit children and adults confined to institutions. The Holiday Project is in approximately 400 communities.

Write: The Holiday Project, P. O. Box 6829, Dept. R, FDR Station, New York, NY 10150 -1921 or **Call:** (212) 532-6158.

CHILDREN'S NEEDS IN HOSPITALS

Children in Hospitals is a nonprofit organization dedicated to the education of the public about the needs of children and parents for continued and ample contact when either is hospitalized. It advises parents on how to "shop" for sympathetic doctors and hospitals. It has a publication list of articles such as *We Learned Through Our Son to be Wise Medical Consumers* and *Parents: Consider Yourself Part of the Health Care Team.*

Write: Children in Hospitals, 56 Bellows Hill Road, Carlisle, MA 01741 or **Call:** (508) 369-4467.

MEDICALLY ORIENTED TOYS AND BOOKS

Pediatric Projects, Inc., promotes the mental health of children undergoing health care. It distributes medically oriented therapeutic toys and books for children. Material can be provided to parents about helping children cope with illness, disability, medical treatment, and hospitalization.

Write: Pediatric Projects, Inc. P. O. Box 571555, Tarzana, CA 91357 or **Call:** (818) 705-3660.

SUPPORT FOR THOSE EXPERIENCING THE DEATH OF A CHILD

Perhaps at no other time in life is help more needed than when one experiences the death of a child. Others with a similar experience stand by to talk with those suffering such a loss.

THE COMPASSIONATE FRIENDS

A self-help group of individuals who have experienced the death of a child, brother, or sister. The Compassionate Friends will direct callers to a local chapter to help in coping with a child's death. Schools can contact it for help with a child who has experienced the death of a brother or sister. It has 634 chapters and an international network. Literature and other resources are available.

Write: The Compassionate Friends, P. O. Box 3696, Oak Brook, IL 60522-3696 or **Call:** (708) 990-0010.

> *"Hope ever tells us tomorrow will be better."*
>
> Tibullus

SPECIAL HEALTH-CARE FACILITIES FOR CHILDREN

SPECIAL HEALTH-CARE FACILITIES FOR CHILDREN A number of specialized children hospitals are located throughout the United States. Some of these provide free care for particular children's illnesses.

ST. JUDE CHILDREN'S RESEARCH HOSPITAL

Treats children of all races and creeds without charge, and conducts research on children's catastrophic diseases. Admission by physician's referral only, and primarily limited to children with cancer. Founded by TV star Danny Thomas.
Write: ALSAC-St. Jude Children's Research Hospital, 332 N. Lauderdale, Memphis, TN 38101 or **Call:** (901) 522-0300.

THE JOHNS HOPKINS CHILDREN'S CENTER

The Johns Hopkins Children's Center of the Johns Hopkins Hospital has been treating medical problems of children for over 75 years. It has more than 40 pediatric medical divisions. In addition to the medical care, Johns Hopkins Children's Center includes a comprehensive *Child Life* program to provide play and school activities, live closed-circuit TV shows, and an outdoor play deck or play area. Overnight live-in facilities are provided for parents.
Write: Johns Hopkins Children's Center, 600 N. Wolfe Street, Baltimore, MD 21205 or **Call:** (301) 955-2000.

THE CHILDREN'S HOUSE AT JOHNS HOPKINS

The Children's House at Johns Hopkins is a four-level, 18-unit facility designed as a warm home away from home for families and out-patient children being treated in the Johns Hopkins Children's Center. The House also serves as the headquarters for the many pediatric support groups within the hospital.
Write: The Grant-A-Wish Foundation, P. O. Box 21211, Baltimore, MD 21228 or **Call:** (301) 242-1549; (800) 933-5470.

NATIONAL JEWISH CENTER FOR IMMUNOLOGY AND RESPIRATORY MEDICINE Provides care, treatment, and rehabilitation of intractable asthmatic children of all races and creeds from all parts of the U. S., Canada, and other nations.
Write: National Jewish Center for Immunology and Respiratory Medicine, 1400 Jackson Street, Denver, CO 80206 or **Call:** (800) 222-LUNG.

SHRINER'S HOSPITAL FOR CHILDREN
Provides free care for children under 18 needing orthopedic and burn treatment. There are 22 hospitals. This is a referral line, and applications and information are available upon request.
Call: (800) 237-5055; Florida (800) 282-9161.

SAMMY DAVIS, JR., NATIONAL LIVER INSTITUTE
The Sammy Davis, Jr., National Liver Institute is the first national medical resource center devoted solely to patient care, education, and research for disease and disorders of the liver and biliary tract. Affiliated with the University of Medicine and Dentistry of New Jersey. The institute (1) renders patient care through a referral clinic and inpatient service; (2) provides up-to-date information on diseases of the liver and biliary tract; and (3) supports research on mechanisms responsible for liver disease, and the development of specific preventive, diagnostic, and therapeutic measures.
Write: Sammy Davis, Jr., National Liver Institute, 185 South Orange Avenue, Medical Science Building, I-506, Newark, NJ 07103-2757 or **Call:** (201) 456-4535/7291.

"No one really knows enough to be a pessimist."

Norman Cousins

CITY OF HOPE/CANCER AND MAJOR DISEASES CENTER Offers quality care, research, and medical second opinions to cancer, leukemia, heart, blood, and lung-disease victims.
Write: City of Hope, 1500 East Duarte Road, Duarte, CA 91010 or **Call:** (800) 423-7119.

CHILDREN'S HOSPICE INTERNATIONAL
This group promotes hospice support in pediatric-care facilities. A number of helpful publications and videotapes are available.
Write: Children's Hospice International, 901 N. Washington Street, Suite 700, Alexandria, VA 22314 or **Call:** (800) 24 CHILD, (703) 684-0330.

LITTLE CITY FOR RETARDED CHILDREN
A national provider of services to children and adults with mental retardation and other developmental challenges. The foundation provides residential, educational, vocational, recreational, and health and wellness services.
Write: Little City for Retarded Children, 4801 West Peterson, Chicago, IL 60646 or **Call:** (312) 282-2207.

JOIN NIH STUDIES
If your child has an illness that is being studied by the National Institutes of Health, it may admit him or her as a patient. Such patients receive free medical care.
Write: Director of the Clinical Center, Building 10, Room 2C146, National Institutes of Health, Bethesda, MD 20892 or **Call:** NIH, Warren Grant Magnuson Clinical Center's Patient Referral Services Unit (301) 496-4891.

FREE MEDICAL CARE AND ADVICE

With escalating medical costs it is good to know that there are some places where you can receive free help.

FREE OR LOW-COST MEDICAL CARE

Over 2,600 medical care facilities participate in the Federal Hill-Burton Free Care Program. A free brochure describing eligibility requirements is available.

Call: Hotline: (800) 638-0742; MD(800) 492-0359.

> *"Real love stories never have endings."*
>
> Richard Bach

5

CHILDREN'S MENTAL HEALTH AND MENTAL RETARDATION

GENERAL INFORMATION ON CHILDREN'S MENTAL HEALTH

Clearinghouses and publications exist that will lead you in the right direction for answers to your specific questions on children's mental health and mental retardation.

MENTAL HEALTH

The National Institute of Mental Health can provide you with information and publications on child mental health. The following publications are available: *Plain Talk About Dealing with the Angry Child* (ADM 79-781); *Plain Talk About Raising Children* (ADM 79-875); and *Plain Talk About When Your Child Starts School* (ADM 80-1021).

Write: National Institute of Mental Health, Information Resources and Inquiries Branch, 5600 Fishers Lane, Room 15C-05, Rockville, MD 20857 or **Call:** (301) 443-4513; (301) 443-4514.

FAMILIES FOR CHILDREN'S MENTAL HEALTH

The Federation of Families for Children's Mental Health provides an opportunity for family members to work with professionals and others interested in improving services for children with emotional, behavioral, or mental disorders.

Write: Federation of Families for Children's Mental Health, 1021 Prince Street, Alexandria, VA 22314-2971 or **Call:** (703) 684-7710.

MENTALLY ILL YOUTH NETWORK

The National Alliance for the Mentally Ill has a Children and Adolescents Network which provides support, information, and advocacy for parents of mentally ill and /or seriously emotionally disturbed children and adolescents.

Write: NAMI, 2101 Wilson Boulevard, Suite 302, Arlington, VA 22201 or **Call:** (703) 524-7600.

GUIDE TO MENTAL HEALTH SERVICES

The government can send you a free publication, *A Consumer's Guide to Mental Health Services* (541X), which answers commonly asked questions on mental health and the different methods of treatment.

Write: Consumer Information Center, Dept. 541X, Pueblo CO 81009.

NATIONAL SELF-HELP CLEARINGHOUSE

Self-help groups are an effective means of dealing with difficult problems. A national clearinghouse can help you find a particular group which addresses your problem or that of a student or friend.

Write: National Self-Help Clearinghouse, 25 West 43rd Street, Room 620, New York, NY 10036 or **Call:** (212) 642-2944.

DEALING WITH STRESS

Stress is taking a major toll among our young people. The National Institutes of Mental Health can send you a free booklet, *Plain Talk About Stress,* which tell you how to effectively deal with stress.

Write: Consumer Information Center, Dept. 544X, Pueblo, CO 81009.

MUTUAL HELP GROUPS

Many support groups exist to give you strength by sharing your problems with others. The National Institutes of Mental Health can send you a overview of the various support groups available entitled *Plain Talk About Mutual Help Groups*.
Write: Consumer Information Center, Dept. 553W, Pueblo, CO 81002.

PHOBIAS: FEAR AND LOATHING

Victims of phobias suffer intense anxiety about objects or situations that pose no real threat to their safety. A free booklet is available entitled *Phobic & Panic Disorders: Getting Help*.
Write: Phobia Society of America/Dept. H, P.O. Box 42514, Washington, DC 20015-05141.

MENTAL HEALTH TAPES

Excellent cassette tapes are available for $6.95 called *Going With Your Feelings – On Track Or Derailed?* and *What Are We Teaching Our Children –Reality, Morality, Responsibility?* They can help parents understand what **feelings** are about and assist them in helping a child deal with his or her feelings constructively.
Write: Study Tapes International, 1345 Pine Knoll, Redlands, CA 92373.

ANXIETY DISORDERS ASSOCIATION OF AMERICA

Young people can suffer from a variety of phobias. The ADAA serves as a clearinghouse for resources and self-help groups to treat this disorder.
Write: ADAA Anxiety Disorders Association of America, 6000 Executive Blvd., Rockville, MD 20852 or **Call:** (301) 231-9350.

COPING WITH DEPRESSION

The National Foundation for Depressive Illness provides a recorded message that describes the symptoms of depression and gives an address for more information and physician referral.
Call: (800) 248-4344.

WHAT TO DO WHEN A FRIEND IS DEPRESSED

The National Institute of Mental Health can send you a free publication describing what a teenager can do if a friend is depressed. Ask for *What To Do When A Friend Is Depressed: A Guide For Teenagers* (10M 88-4036).

Write: Public Inquiries Branch, Room 15C-05, Office of Scientific Information, National Institute of Mental Health, 5600 Fishers Lane, Rockville, MD 20857 or **Call:** (301) 443-4513.

ATTENTION-DEFICIT DISORDERS

Some children have a disorder characterized by deficits in attention span and impulse control, which is frequently accompanied by hyperactivity. An organization can provide parents and teachers support and educational material for dealing with this problem.

Write: Children with Attention-Deficit Disorders, 499 N.W. 70th Avenue, Suite 308, Plantation, FL 33317 or **Call:** (305) 587-3700.

QUESTIONS ON SCHIZOPHRENIA

Confusion surrounds this mental disease. A free publication entitled *Schizophrenia: Questions And Answers* (546X), by the National Institute of Mental Health describes the causes, treatments, and outlook for this debilitating illness affecting millions of Americans.

Write: Consumer Information Center, Dept. 546X, Pueblo, CO 81009.

CREATIVE THERAPEUTICS

This organization can send you a catalog of literature to assist children in dealing with various life issues such as divorce, adoption, illness, and emotional problems.

Write: Creative Therapeutics, P. O. Box R, Cresskill, NJ 07626 or **Call:** (800) 544-6162; (201) 567-7295.

WISCONSIN CLEARINGHOUSE

This agency of the University of Wisconsin can provide you with a free catalog of hundreds of resources on alcohol and other drug abuse, prevention, and mental health. It is interested in youth development, school health and wellness, and women's issues. A booklet entitled *Adolescence and Depression* is available for $1.00. Also available: the Children at Risk Series of research reviews.

Write: Wisconsin Clearinghouse, P. O. Box 1468, Madison, WI 53701-1468 or **Call:** (800) 322-1468; (608) 263-2797.

EATING DISORDERS We are just beginning to understand the nature of these disorders, but a number of organizations can give you the latest information and provide support.

ANAD - NATIONAL ASSOCIATION OF ANOREXIA NERVOSA

Anorexics, bulimics, their families, and health care professionals interested in the problem of anorexia nervosa and bulimia. ANAD maintain a speakers' bureau, provides children's services, and conducts a referral service.

Write: ANAD - National Association of Anorexia Nervosa and Associated Disorders, P. O. Box 7, Highland Park, IL 60035 or **Call:** (708) 831-3438.

AMERICAN ANOREXIA /BULIMIA ASSOCIATION

This organization is composed of families and professionals interested in these eating disorders. It is a nonprofit, self-help group which acts as an information and referral service for people dealing with these problems.

Write: American Anorexia/Bulimia Association, 418 E. 76th Street, New York, NY 10021 or **Call:** (212) 734-1114.

BASH, SELF-HELP FOR ANOREXICS AND BULIMICS

Self-help group of individuals coping with bulimia (binging and purging) and anorexia (self-induced starvation). BASH provides a 24-hour crisis-intervention hotline and will mail information to you free of charge. Not a referral service.

Write: BASH, 6125 Clayton Avenue, Suite 215, St. Louis, MO 63139 or **Call:** Crisis Hotline (314) 768-3292 (24 hr.); M0 (800) 768-3838; BASH Information (800) 227-4785, M-F 9 a.m.– 5 p.m.

OVEREATERS ANONYMOUS

A national fellowship of individuals who, through shared experience and mutual support, are recovering from compulsive overeating. OA welcomes anyone who wants to stop eating compulsively. There are no dues or fees for membership.

Write: Overeaters Anonymous, Inc., 4025 Spencer Street, #203, Torrance, CA 90503 or **Call:** (213) 618-8835.

CHILDHOOD OBESITY

A free government publication is available entitled *Obesity in Childhood*, which describes approaches for solving this problem.

Write: Office of Research Reporting, National Institute of Child Health and Human Development, Building 31, Room 2A-32, National Institutes of Health, 9000 Rockville Pike, Bethesda, MD 20892 or **Call:** (301) 496-5133.

> *"Everybody needs to be* **somebody.** *It's a basic human need."*
>
> **Dr. Richard Nies**

CHILDREN WITH MENTAL RETARDATION

Fortunately, a number of people and organizations are available to assist mentally retarded children.

AMERICAN ASSOCIATION ON MENTAL RETARDATION

An association of professionals and concerned individuals in the field of mental retardation. AAMR promotes the well-being of individuals with mental retardation and supports those who work in the field. It promotes quality services for those with mental retardation and their families. Information on the cause, treatment, and prevention of mental retardation is available.

Write: American Association on Mental Retardation, 1719 Kalorama Road, N.W., Washington, DC 20009 or **Call:** (202) 387-1968.

LEARNING DISABILITIES ASSOCIATION OF AMERICA

This association provides assistance to parents, children, schools, camps, and recreational programs. It serves as a clearinghouse for problems associated with children's learning disabilities and distributes publications on this subject.

Write: Learning Disabilities Association of America, 4156 Library Road, Pittsburgh, PA 15234 or **Call:** (412) 341-1515.

ASSOCIATION FOR RETARDED CITIZENS

Serves six million children and adults with mental retardation and their families. Can put you in touch with local help.

Write: Association for Retarded Citizens, 500 E. Border Street, 3rd Floor, Arlington, TX 76010 or **Call:** (817) 261-6003.

SPECIAL OLYMPICS INTERNATIONAL

Special Olympics provides year-round sports training and athletic competition in a variety of olympic-type sports for all children and adults with mental retardation.

Write: Special Olympics International, 1350 New York, N.W., Suite 500, Washington, DC 20005 or **Call:** (202) 628-3630.

AUTISM The autistic child presents special communication and behavioral problems. Individuals and programs are available to help.

CHILDREN AND ADULTS WITH AUTISM

The Autism Society of America (ASA) is a charitable organization with the mission of providing as much information as possible about autism, and about the various options, approaches, methods, and systems available to parents of autistic children, family members, and those professionals who work with them. ASA also advocates for the rights and needs of autistic individuals and their families.
Write: Autism Society of America, 8601 Georgia Avenue, Suite 503, Silver Spring, MD 20910 or **Call:** (301) 565-0433.

SOCIETY FOR AUTISTIC CHILDREN

An organization of people concerned about the welfare of children with severe disorders of communication and behavior. It can provide a directory of services and programs for autistic children.
Write: New York State Society for Autistic Children, 879 Madison Avenue, Albany, NY 12208 or **Call:** (518) 459-1418.

AUTISM SERVICES CENTER

Assists families and agencies with the difficult and unique needs of clients who are autistic. Can provide a free packet with information on autism plus individualized assistance.
Write: Autism Services Center, The Prichard Building, 605 Ninth Street, P. O. Box 507, Huntington, WV 25710-0507 or **Call:** (304) 525-8014.

> *"It has been well said that our anxiety does not empty tomorrow of its sorrows, but only empties today of its strength."* **Spurgeon**

DOWN SYNDROME Children with Down Syndrome have special needs as do the people who love and care for them. A number of support groups and organizations exist with programs which will help.

PARENTS OF DOWN SYNDROME CHILDREN

This group can send you a Parent Information Kit and provide suggestions for support services.
Write: Parents of Down Syndrome Children, c/o Mongomery County Association for Retarded Citizens, 11600 Nebel Street, Rockville, MD 20852 or **Call:** (301) 984-5792.

NATIONAL DOWN SYNDROME CONGRESS

An organization dedicated to improving the quality of life for people born with Down Syndrome. The Congress can answer your questions on this disorder, send you literature, and refer you to local help.
Write: National Down Syndrome Congress, 1800 Dempster Street, Park Ridge, IL 60068-1146 or **Call:** (800) 232-6372; (708) 823-7550.

NATIONAL DOWN SYNDROME SOCIETY

Five thousand babies a year are born with Down Syndrome. The National Down Syndrome Society maintains a hotline to answer questions on this disorder and to refer parents to medical facilities, counseling services, and educational material. A free informational packet and videocassette, *Gift of Love*, are available on request.
Write: National Down Syndrome Society, 666 Broadway, Suite 810, New York, NY 10012 or **Call:** (800) 221-4602.

6

CHILDREN WITH DISABILITIES

GENERAL INFORMATION SOURCES

Agencies and individuals stand by to help children with disabilities. They can sometimes make the difference between a burdensome or productive life.

HOTLINE FOR CHILDREN AND YOUTH WITH DISABILITIES A National Information Center for Children and Youth with Disabilities is maintained to help professionals, teachers, advocates, and parents of children with disabilities. This information center can answer questions regarding your child and put you in touch with local help. Free literature is available describing various disabilities and ways of educating a child with disabilities.

Write: National Information for Children and Youth with Disabilities, P. O. Box 1492, Washington, DC 20013 or **Call:** (703) 893-6061; toll free (800) 999-5599 ; TDD (703) 893-8614.

BOOKS ABOUT DISABILITIES

Special Needs Projects offers many excellent books about physical and mental disabilities (particularly children's). Hospitalization and general health, and other books about parenting are listed in a free catalog.

Write: Special Needs Project, 1482 E. Valley Road, #A121, Santa Barbara, CA 93108 or **Call:** (805) 565-1914; Toll-free order phone (800) 333-6867.

DISABILITIES CLEARINGHOUSE

A national clearinghouse exists which can answer your questions about a child with disabilities and put you in touch with people who can give you added assistance. The clearinghouse responds to inquiries on a wide range of topics. Information is especially strong in the areas of federal funding for programs serving disabled people, federal legislation affecting the disabled community, and federal programs benefiting people with disabling conditions. A publication, *Pocket Guide to Federal Help for Individuals With Disabilities*, is available.

Write: Clearinghouse for Disability Information, 330 C Street, S.W., Washington, DC 20202-2524 or **Call:** (202) 732-1245.

CENTER FOR PERSONS WITH DISABILITIES

The purpose of this center is to improve the quality of life for persons with disabilities and their families. Programs are in progress to help achieve this goal, including direct-service programs for clients of all ages, research projects, and a large technical assistance network aimed at improving the quality of services provided by many different agencies. Another primary aim is to provide interdisciplinary training to persons associated with persons with disabilities.

Write: Center for Persons With Disabilities, UMC, Utah State University, Logan, UT 84322-6800 or **Call:** (801) 750-1981.

SIBLING INFORMATION NETWORK

Serves as a clearinghouse for research and services regarding siblings of persons with developmental disabilities.

Write: Sibling Information Network, A. J. Pappanikou Center on Special Education and Rehabilitation: A University Affiliated Program, 991 Main Street, East Hartford, CT 06108 or **Call:** (203) 282-7050.

WHAT IT FEELS LIKE TO BE DISABLED

Children need not be frightened or timid when they meet a person with a disability. A little education can break down the barriers. *Each & Every One* is a program which brings puppets that represent children with differences and disabilities into classrooms.

Write: Kids on the Block, 9385 C. Gerwig Lane, Columbia, MD 21046 or **Call:** (800) 368-KIDS.

SPORTS AND RECREATION FOR THE DISABLED

Athletics can often mean more to handicapped young people than to the able-bodied, and competition can be just as keen.

NATIONAL HANDICAPPED SPORTS

NHS provides nationwide, year-round sports and recreation programs for children and adults with orthopedic, spinal cord, neuromuscular, and visual impairments.

Write: National Handicapped Sports, 4405 East-West Highway, Suite 603, Bethesda, MD 20814 or **Call:** (301) 652-7505.

SPECIAL RECREATION, INC.

An organization that promotes self-determination and normalization in recreational activities and leisure for disabled individuals. It can send you a catalog of special recreational services for disabled individuals and publishes a quarterly and annual recreational digest.

Write: Special Recreation, Inc., 362 Koser Avenue, Iowa City, IA 52246 or **Call:** (319) 337-7578.

PHYSICALLY IMPAIRED CHILDREN

The special needs of disabled children are the concerns of a number of organizations.

ASSOCIATION FOR THE SEVERELY HANDICAPPED

This association publishes a monthly newsletter and a quarterly journal that reports current innovations and research for persons who are severely handicapped. It has publications and makes referrals.
Write: The Association for Persons With Severe Handicaps, 7010 Roosevelt Way, N. E., Seattle, WA 98115 or **Call:** (206) 523-8446.

NATIONAL EASTER SEAL SOCIETY, INC.

Provides information and referral for persons with disabilities, their families, and friends on services available, and research and technological assistance.
Write: National Easter Seal Society, Inc., 70 Eastlake Street, Chicago, IL 60601 or **Call:** (312) 726-6200 (8:30 a.m.-5 p.m. CST).

MARCH OF DIMES BIRTH DEFECTS FOUNDATION

This foundation can supply films, filmstrips, exhibits, and educational material on birth defects.
Write: March of Dimes Birth Defects Foundation, National Headquarters, 1275 Mamaroneck Avenue, White Plains, NY 10605 or **Call:** (914) 997-4636.

SCHOOL REINTEGRATION PROGRAM

Loma Linda University Medical Center has a program to help children with a physical handicap from illness or injury (permanent or temporary) reintegrate into the school system. Personnel go to the schools and help train the staff and teachers to deal with the specific needs of the child. Loma Linda University will provide information on how to set up a similar program in your area.
Write: Child Life Program, Loma Linda University Medical Center, 11234 Anderson Street, Loma Linda, CA 92354 or **Call:** (714) 824-0800, Ext. 6555.

CRANIOFACIAL DISORDERS

A number of craniofacial problems require special technology to correct them. Most notable among such problems is a cleft palate.

CLEFT PALATE/CRANIOFACIAL BIRTH DEFECTS

The Cleft Palate Foundation operates a toll-free CLEFTLINE for parents with children born with cleft lip, palate, and other craniofacial birth defects. Referrals are made to cleft palate/craniofacial health-care teams and to parent-support groups. Free information is available to parents. Quarterly newsletter is available.
Write: Cleft Palate Foundation, 1218 Grandview Avenue, Pittsburgh, PA 15211 or **Call:** (800) 24-CLEFT; PA.

DWARFS

Organizations of little people exist to address the special problems encountered by dwarfs.

LITTLE PEOPLE OF AMERICA

Dwarfs, including children, can become part of this organization. It operates to provide fellowship, moral support, and problem-solving ideas to little people. Little People of America has a medical advisory board and is affiliated with the Little People of America Foundation. It publishes a booklet *My Child Is A Dwarf* and has parent-support groups for parents of dwarf children.
Write: Little People of America, P. O. Box 9897, Washington, DC 20016 or **Call:** (301) 589-0730.

LITTLE PEOPLE RESEARCH FUND

This organization supports research, education, and patient care. Its focus is the disabling orthopedic impairments associated with dwarfism. This research fund is international in scope.
Write: Little People Research Fund, 80 Sister Pierre Drive, Towson, MD 21204 or **Call:** (301) 494-0055; (800) 232-LPRF.

SPEECH AND LANGUAGE DISORDERS

The causes of these difficulties can be varied. It is important that they be diagnosed and treated early.

NATIONAL CENTER FOR STUTTERING

Distributes information for parents of young children showing early signs of stuttering. For older children and adults free information is available on treatment programs nationwide.
Write: National Center for Stuttering, 200 E. 33 Street, New York, NY 10016 or **Call:** (800) 221-2483; (212) 532-1460.

SPEECH AND LANGUAGE DISORDERS

The National Institutes of Health have prepared a booklet entitled *Development Speech and Language Disorders* (50¢). It discusses speaking and understanding problems children have. A chart of language milestones from ages 1 to 6 is included.
Write: Consumer Information Center, Department 448X, Pueblo, CO 81009.

CLEARINGHOUSES FOR STUTTERERS

Three major clearinghouses for stuttering literature, self-help groups, and referrals for local help are:
Write: National Council on Stuttering, Box 40742, Indianapolis, IN 46240-0742.
Write: National Stuttering Project, 4601 Irving Street, San Francisco, CA 94122-1020 or **Call:** (415) 566-5324.
Write: Speak Easy International Foundation, 233 Concord Drive, Paramus, NJ 07652 or **Call:** (201) 262-0895.

> *"I have learned silence from the talkative; tolerance from the intolerant and kindness from the unkind. I should not be ungrateful to those teachers."*
>
> Kahlil Gibran

ADAPTIVE CLOTHES AND DEVICES FOR CHILDREN WITH DISABILITIES

Technical devices and special clothing are available that can enhance the quality of life for children with disabilities.

CENTER FOR SPECIAL EDUCATION TECHNOLOGY

This group can provide you with information on using modern technology for children with disabilities.

Write: Center for Special Education Technology, CEC, 1920 Association Drive, Reston, VA 22091 or **Call:** (800) 873-8255; (703) 620-3660.

SPECIAL CLOTHES FOR SPECIAL CHILDREN

Special clothing for handicapped children from toddlers to young adults. Everything from trousers to jackets and hats. They can send you a catalog. Clothes can be custom designed and made for special problems.

Write: Special Clothes for Special Children, P.O. Box 4220, Alexandria, VA 22303 or **Call:** (703) 683-7343.

PROJECTS FOR SPECIAL CHILDREN

These people are set up to distribute practical products for needy children with handicaps. They distribute adaptive clothing and toys and other kinds of equipment to needy handicapped children. Clothing, toys, and equipment are donated through other nonprofit agencies.

Write: Projects for Special Children, 20 W. Masonic View Avenue, Alexandria, VA 22301 or **Call:** (703) 549-2640.

TOYS FOR SPECIAL CHILDREN

A group which adapts toys with special switches for those special children who need them. Catalog is available upon request for $3.00. Also, a video catalog showing the devices and switches can be obtained for $6.50.

Write: Toys for Special Children, Inc., c/o Steven Kanor, Ph. D., 385 Warburton Avenue, Hastings-on-Hudson, NY 10706 or **Call:** (914) 478-0960.

CHILDREN WHO ARE BLIND

Children who are blind have special needs. Many organizations are dedicated to helping them lead happy and successful lives.

AMERICAN FOUNDATION FOR THE BLIND

National research, information, and consultative agency that acts as a clearinghouse for local and regional agencies serving the blind. It operates a hotline which supplies information on visual impairment and blindness and answers queries. You may request a products catalog which contains such items as Braille Monopoly and a talking calculator. Pamphlets are available, entitled *Parenting Preschoolers; Suggestions for Raising Young Blind and Visually Impaired Children*; and *Touch the Baby.*

Write: American Foundation for the Blind, 15 W. 16th Street, New York, NY 10011 or **Call:** (800) AFB-LIND; (800) 232-5463; NY (212) 620-2147.

EYE BANK FOR SIGHT RESTORATION

Collects and distributes healthy corneal tissue. Associated with Eye-Bank Association of America.

Write: Eye Bank for Sight Restoration, 210 East 64th Street, New York, NY 10021 or **Call:** (212) 980-6700.

BLIND CHILDREN'S CENTER

These people have developed an educational correspondence course that is free to families with visually handicapped preschool children. The primary goal of the course is to teach parents to facilitate their child's achievement of successive developmental milestones in the following areas: (1) sensory-motor development; (2) language; (3) cognitive development; (4) affective development; and (5) socialization and self-help skills.

Write: Blind Children's Center, 4120 Marathon Street, P.O. Box 29159-0159, Los Angeles, CA 90029 or **Call:** (213) 664-2153.

NATIONAL FEDERATION OF THE BLIND

The National Federation of the Blind is a self-help and advocacy organization providing blind individuals with scholarships, employment assistance, civil rights protection, Braille, and recorded publications. A publication for parents of blind children, called *Future Reflections*, is available. It has a Parents of Blind Children Division.
Write: National Federation of the Blind, 1800 Johnson Street, Baltimore, MD 21230 or **Call:** (301) 659-9314.

RECORDING FOR THE BLIND

National nonprofit service providing free educational books to blind and other print-handicapped individuals in the U. S. and abroad.
Write: Recording for the Blind, 20 Roszel Road, Princeton, NJ 08540 or **Call:** (609) 452-0606.

GUIDEDOG FOUNDATION FOR THE BLIND

The Guidedog Foundation for the Blind, Inc., provides blind rehabilitation, without charge to recipients, through guide dogs and residential training.
Write: Guidedog Foundation for the Blind, 371 E. Jericho Turnpike, Smithtown, NY 11787 or **Call:** (800) 548-4337; (516) 265-2121.

HI-TECH FOR BLIND CHILDREN

You can call these people for information or to request a catalog on the latest devices to help a blind child (Braille watches, games, and the like). Free brochures are available on topics such as *What Do You Do When You See a Blind Person?* and *Products for People With Vision Problems*.
Write: Consumer Products Division, American Foundation for the Blind, 15 W. 16th Street, New York, NY 10011 or **Call:** (212) 620-2171; (212) 620-2172.

VISUALLY IMPAIRED CHILDREN A multitude of services is available to the visually impaired young person. A number of resources are listed:

NATIONAL ASSOCIATION FOR PARENTS OF THE VISUALLY IMPAIRED An organization that provides support, information, and services for parents of visually-impaired children. A quarterly newsletter called *Awareness* is available.
Write: National Association for Parents of the Visually Impaired, 2180 Linway Drive, Beloit, WI 53511 or **Call:** (800) 562-6265.

LARGE-PRINT BOOKS FOR CHILDREN
Grey Castle Books produces large-print books for young people with impaired vision—including *Nancy Drew*, *The Hardy Boys*, and Choose Your Own Adventure series.
Write: Grey Castle Press, Pocket Knife Square, Lakeville, CT 06039 or **Call:** (203) 435-2518; (FAX) (203) 435-8093.
Cornerstone Books offers large-print books for children 8-15 years. They also have large-print Read Alongs – a special combination of complete and unabridged titles – for students with special needs.
Write: Cornerstone Books, a Division of ABC-CLIO, 130 Cremona, Box 1911, Santa Barbara, CA 93116-1911 or **Call:** (800) 422-2546.

NATIONAL ASSOCIATION FOR THE VISUALLY HANDICAPPED An organization solely devoted to serving over 11 million partially seeing individuals. Distributes information, large-print materials, visual aids, and offers referrals, and public and professional education programs.
Write: NAVH, 22 West 21st Street, New York, NY 10010 or **Call:** (212) 889-3141. Also **Write:** (for the 13 western states, Alaska, and Hawaii) NAVH, 3201 Balboa Street, San Francisco, CA 94121 or **Call:** (415) 221-8753.

RETINITIS PIGMENTOSA FOUNDATION

Retinitis pigmentosa is a degenerative disease usually beginning with night blindness in children. This organization is dedicated to finding an understanding of the causes of retinal degeneration diseases and stimulating the development of a treatment. A national registry is maintained for those afflicted with retinal degeneration.

Write: National Retinitis Pigmentosa Foundation, 1401 Mount Royal Avenue, Baltimore, MD 21217 or **Call:** (800) 638-2300; (301) 225-9400.

NATIONAL SOCIETY TO PREVENT BLINDNESS

The society's mission is to prevent blindness through on-site screening, education, industrial, and sports eye-safety programs. Twenty-five affiliates serve the U.S. Produces publications such as the *Family Home Eye Test and Your Child's Sight.* Single copies are free.

Write: National Society to Prevent Blindness, 500 East Remington Road, Schaumburg, IL 60173 or **Call:** (800) 221-3004.

HELEN KELLER NATIONAL CENTER FOR DEAF–BLIND YOUTHS AND ADULTS

This organization acts as a national resource center. It is the single, national program which provides diagnostic evaluation, short-term comprehensive rehabilitation training and job preparation and placement for Americans who are deaf/blind from every state and territory. This center can send you a *Directory of Agencies Serving the Deaf-Blind* (for $15.00, prepaid). Conducts extensive network of field services through regional offices, affiliated programs and a National Training Team.

Write: Helen Keller National Center for Deaf-Blind Youths and Adults, 111 Middle Neck Road, Sands Point, NY 11050 or **Call:** (516) 944-8900 (Voice/TDD).

CHILDREN WHO ARE DEAF

The deaf child must be equipped with the special communication skills and aids that are available.

AMERICAN SOCIETY FOR DEAF CHILDREN

A parent-support organization that provides information and encouragement to families with deaf children. It supports the philosophy of total communication and attempts to promote a positive attitude in the community towards deafness, sign language, and deaf people. Its ultimate goal is quality education for deaf children.
Write: American Society for Deaf Children, 814 Thayer Avenue, Silver Spring, MD 20910 or **Call:** (301) 585-5400 (Voice/TDD).

PARENTS OF DEAF CHILDREN

As part of the Alexander Graham Bell Association for the Deaf, there is a parents' organization that is concerned with the educational, social, and psychological needs of hearing-impaired children. Parents of Deaf Children has publications on the problems of deaf children. Financial-aid programs are available for profoundly hearing-impaired oral children from infants through college.
Write: Information Services, Alexander Graham Bell Association for the Deaf, 3417 Volta Pl., N. W., Washington, DC 20007 or **Call:** (202) 337-5220.

DEAFPRIDE, INC.

Deafpride has a variety of programs: *Project Access*–to help deaf women and families ensure their access to health care. Interpreting services are available 24 hours a day. *Project AIDS*–provides education and training on AIDS to the deaf community and insures accessibility to AIDS-treatment programs. *Project: A Second Chance*–alcohol and chemical dependency services. *Sign Language*– provides sign-language classes and tutoring to individuals and organizations.
Write: Deafpride, Inc., 1350 Potomac Avenue, S.E., Washington, DC 20003 or **Call:** (202) 675-6700 (Voice/TTY).

PROJECT: A SECOND CHANCE

Deafpride works with deaf persons who are recovering from addiction to drugs and alcohol. Staff work to make treatment and aftercare programs accessible to deaf persons and their families.

Write: Deafpride, Inc., 1350 Potomac Avenue, S.E., Washington, DC 20003 or **Call:** (202) 675-6700 (Voice/TTY).

ALEXANDER GRAHAM BELL ASSOCIATION FOR THE DEAF

This organization promotes the teaching of speech and lipreading and offers scholarships for oral deaf students (infants-college age).

Write: Alexander Graham Bell Association for the Deaf, 3417 Volta Place, N.W., Washington, DC 20007 or **Call:** (202) 337-5220.

MODERN TALKING PICTURE SERVICE, INC.

This organization provides a free-loan captioned film/video program for the deaf. This service seeks to afford for deaf/hearing-impaired persons the same understanding and appreciation of films that are enjoyed by hearing persons. The loan service is funded by the U.S. Department of Education. The only expense to the user is postage to return the films. Videocassettes have prepaid postage. A catalog is supplied upon request. Enclosed with each film/video are lesson guides that provide teachers information on its use. To receive a catalog you must apply for an account and be approved.

Write: Modern Talking Picture Service, Inc., 5000 Park Street, N., St. Petersburg, FL 33709 or **Call:** (800) 237-6213 (Voice/TTY); (813) 545-8781 (Voice/TTY).

> *"Kindness is a language which the deaf can hear and the blind can read."* **Mark Twain**

REGISTRY OF INTERPRETERS FOR THE DEAF, INC.

Maintains a registry of certified interpreters for the deaf. It also publishes books and publications relating to the profession of interpreting for the deaf. **Write:** Registry of Interpreters for the Deaf, Inc., 8719 Colesville Road, Suite 310, Silver Spring, MD 20910 or **Call:** (301) 608-0050 (V/TTY).

INTERNATIONAL HEARING DOGS, INC.

An organization that trains and places dogs, free of charge, with deaf individuals who have reached independence and are living alone or with other hearing-impaired individuals. Deaf children just starting on their own may call. Priorities are: 65-decibel loss, living alone or with other hearing-impaired persons, no other dog, and must be mentally and physically capable of handling a dog. Dogs are also placed with people having multiple handicaps, including blindness and deafness. **Write:** International Hearing Dogs, Inc., 5901 E. 89th Avenue, Henderson, CO 80640 or **Call:** (303) 287-3277.

NATIONAL CAPTIONING INSTITUTE

Provides captioning for the hearing-impaired, deaf children and adults so that with the help of a decoder, they can read the dialog of certain TV programs home videocassettes, and cable. The captioning is also useful for children with learning disabilities and English as a second language. **Write:** National Captioning Institute, 5203 Leesburg Pike, Falls Church, VA 22041 or **Call:** (703) 998-2400 (Voice or TTY).

> *"The only courage that matters is the kind that gets you from one moment to the next."*
>
> **Mignon McLaughlin**

HEARING-IMPAIRED CHILDREN

The special needs of hearing-impaired children and young people can be met through a variety of programs and services.

ASSESSMENT CENTER FOR HEARING-IMPAIRED CHILDREN AND YOUTH

The assessment center serves as a model diagnostic program which supplements a number of ongoing Kendall School outreach activities through dissemination of methods, materials, and research findings related to the assessment of the hearing-impaired population.

Write: Jean Moore, Coordinator, Assessment Center for Hearing-Impaired Children and Youth, Kendall Demonstration Elementary School, Gallaudet University, 800 Florida Avenue, N.E., Washington, DC 20002 or **Call:** (202) 651-5337; (202) 651-5031 (Voice/TDD).

THE GENETIC SERVICES CENTER (FOR THE DEAF)

Professional genetic services are available for (1) deaf and hard-of-hearing individuals and couples who wish to better understand the cause and future implications of their deafness; (2) parents of deaf and hard-of-hearing children who want information about the cause of their children's hearing loss and the potential for having other children with hearing loss; and (3) individuals with a history of hearing loss in their family who have questions about the effects on future generations. Information on genetic counseling services or referrals for such services.

Write: Kathleen Shaver Arnos, Ph.D., Director, Genetic Services Center, Gallaudet University, 800 Florida Avenue, N.E., c/o MSSD-200, Washington, DC 20002 or **Call:** (800) 451-8834, Ext. 5258 (both Voice/TDD); (202) 651-5258.

GOVERNMENT TDD DIRECTORY

A free publication entitled *U. S. Government TDD Directory* (573X) lists federal agencies that have telecommunications devices for the deaf and how to reach hearing- or speech-impaired federal employees if you don't use a TDD.
Write: Consumer Information Center, Dept. 573X, Pueblo, CO 81009.

PARENTS OF HEARING-IMPAIRED CHILDREN

This is an international organization of parents of hearing-impaired children. It publishes and distributes information concerning the problems of deaf children.
Write: Parents Section, c/o Alexander Graham Bell Association for the Deaf, 3417 Volta Place, N.W., Washington, DC 20007 or **Call:** (202) 337-5220.

EDUCATING A HEARING-IMPAIRED CHILD

TRIPOD Grapevine is an informational and referral service that can answer your questions about educating, rearing, or living with a hearing-impaired child. It can give you a variety of information so that you can make decisions appropriate for your child and family. TRIPOD tries to research personal answers to specific questions, utilizing its worldwide advisory board.
Write: TRIPOD Grapevine, 2901 N. Keystone Street, Burbank, CA 91504 or **Call:** (800) 352-8888; CA (800) 2 TRIPOD.

EDUCATION OF THE HEARING IMPAIRED

The International Organization for the Education of the Hearing Impaired consists of educators of the hearing impaired who are promoting excellence in oral communication. It is a source of the latest research findings in this area.
Write: International Organization for the Education of the Hearing Impaired, c/o Alexander Graham Bell Association for the Deaf, 3417 Volta Pl., N.W., Washington DC 20007 or **Call:** (202) 337-5220 (Voice or TDD).

LEARNING TO SIGN

The Joy of Signing is an illustrated guide for mastering the current basic signs used to communicate with deaf or hearing-impaired people in either the word order of the English language or in the American Sign Language pattern.
Write: Special Needs Project, 1482 E. Valley Road, # A121, Santa Barbara, CA 93108 or **Call:** (805) 565-1914.

VIDEOS ON HEARING-IMPAIRED CHILDREN

TRIPOD Grapevine will loan to parents upon request two excellent videos (open captioned) for families with hearing-impaired children. *Language Says It All* focuses on the importance of establishing clear communication in the home. Parents talk about their concerns for their children; classroom footage of natural child-to-child communication; fairy tales performed in American Sign Language. The second video, *"Once Upon a Time,"* reminds us of how important story time is to parents and their hearing-impaired child. Parents describe the ways in which they learned to share a rich story heritage with their children.
Write: TRIPOD Grapevine, 2901 N. Keystone Street, Burbank, CA 91504 or **Call:** (800) 352-8888; CA (800) 2 TRIPOD.

> *"There are an estimated one million hearing-impaired children in America. Over 90% are born to hearing parents, people with little or no knowledge of deafness."*
>
> *TRIPOD Grapevine, 1990*

7

MATERNAL AND CHILD CARE

GENERAL INFORMATION ON MATERNAL AND CHILD CARE

When to have children and how many to have are questions that are worthy of some deliberation. A national clearinghouse exists that can help you find information on these and other important maternal- and child-care topics.

DIRECTORY OF ORGANIZATIONS RELATED TO MATERNAL AND CHILD CARE The National Center for Education in Maternal and Child Health can send you a directory that provides a listing of over 400 national voluntary, professional, and self-help organizations with a maternal- and child-health focus. A detailed subject index and alphabetical listing of organizations are also provided. Other publications are also available.

Write: The National Maternal and Child Health Clearinghouse, 38th and R Streets, N.W., Washington, DC 20057 or **Call:** (202) 625-8410.

NATIONAL CENTER FOR EDUCATION IN MATERNAL AND CHILD HEALTH The center responds to information requests, maintains a resource center, develops publications, and provides technical assistance in educational resources development, program planning, and topical research in the area of maternal and child health. NCEMCH serves parents, health professionals, voluntary organizations, and local, federal, and state agencies.
Write: National Center for Education in Maternal and Child Health, Georgetown University, 38th and R Streets, N.W., Washington, DC 20057 or **Call:** (202) 625-8400.

DRUGS, ALCOHOL, AND PREGNANCY

More and more infants are born with physical and mental problems linked to the mother's use of alcohol or drugs during pregnancy.

PREVENTING ALCOHOL-RELATED BIRTH DEFECTS
The body of knowledge gained through clinical reports and experimental studies in the past 12 years clearly shows that alcohol is associated with a variety of adverse fetal outcomes. The Department of Health and Human Services has a publication (DHHS No. [ADM] 85-151) which comprehensively covers this subject.
Write: National Center for Education in Maternal and Child Health, Georgetown University, 38th and R Streets, N.W., Washington, DC 20057 or **Call:** (202) 625-8400.

EFFECTS OF ALCOHOL ON PREGNANCY
Free publications are available that discuss the effects of alcohol on pregnancy. They are *Fetal Alcohol Syndrome* and *The Fact Is Alcohol and Other Drugs Can Harm an Unborn Baby* .
Write: National Clearinghouse for Alcohol Information, P. O. Box 2345, Rockville, MD 20852 or **Call:** (301) 468-2600.

HEALTH OF THE MOTHER

The health of the mother during pregnancy profoundly affects the health of the newborn.

HEALTHY MOTHERS, HEALTHY BABIES

A national, nonprofit coalition comprised of 95 professional, voluntary, and governmental organizations that share ideas and information on issues such as prenatal care, nutrition for pregnant women, and infant mortality. It is also concerned with adolescent pregnancy, breast-feeding, genetics, and injury prevention. Resource material is available on request.
Write: Healthy Mothers, Healthy Babies, 409 12th Street, S.W., Room 309, Washington, DC 20024-2188 or **Call:** (202) 863-2458.

LAMAZE CHILDBIRTH

The American Society for Psychoprophylaxis in Obstetrics can give you information on Lamaze childbirth preparation and family-centered maternity care. A teacher and physician referral service is provided.
Call: (800) 368-4404; (202) 857-1128.

MULTIPLE BIRTHS

A private, nonprofit center which disseminates information on the medical risks of multiple births and sponsors scientific conferences on twins and other multiples.
Write: Center for Study of Multiple Birth, 333 E. Superior Street, Suite 464, Chicago, IL 60611 or **Call:** (312) 266-9093.

PREGNANCY AFTER 35

A free government publication, *Facts About Down's Syndrome for Women Over 35*, discusses risks of having a Mongoloid child after 35.
Write: Office of Research Reporting, National Institute of Child Health and Human Development, Building 31, Room 2A-32, National Institutes of Health and Human Development, 9000 Rockville Pike, Bethesda, MD 20892 or **Call:** (301) 496-5133.

PREGNANCY AND INFANT LOSS CENTER

Support organization for parents who have suffered a miscarriage, stillbirth, or infant death. It provides literature on pregnancy loss and grief. **Write:** Pregnancy and Infant Loss Center, 1415 E. Wayzata Boulevard, Wayzata, MN 55391 or **Call:** (612) 473-9372.

PROPER NUTRITION FOR INFANT AND CHILD

Knowing and meeting the nutritional needs of your baby and developing child are an important part of your parenting. A variety of organizations and publications can help you.

HOTLINES FOR BABY NUTRITION AND CARE

The major manufacturers of baby foods provide hotlines for questions concerning your baby's nutrition and care. For help:
Call: Beech-Nut Nutrition Hotline (800) 523-6633; Gerber Products Co. (800) 443-7237; and Johnson & Johnson Baby Products Information Center (800) 526-3967.

RESOURCES ON BREAST-FEEDING

The National Center for Education in Maternal and Child Health has two excellent free publications on resources to teach breast-feeding. Ask for *Breast-feeding: Catalog of Products* and *Breast-feeding – Abstracts of Active Projects.*
Write: National Center for Education in Maternal and Child Health, Georgetown University, 38th and R Streets, N.W., Washington, DC 20057 or **Call:** (202) 625-8400.

BREAST-FEEDING

Free government publication entitled *Breast-feeding* (HSA 80-5109), provides information for intelligent decisions concerning breast-feeding and proper techniques.
Write: National Center for Education in Maternal and Child Health, 38th and R Street, N.W., Washington, DC 20057 or **Call:** (202) 625-8400.

LA LECHE LEAGUE INTERNATIONAL

An organization that provides information, support, and encouragement to mothers who want to breast-feed their babies. It can refer you to local chapters. A free catalog of books on breast-feeding is available. It includes a new book that deals with breast-feeding a handicapped child. Local chapters have monthly, guided discussions.
Write: La Leche League International, P. O. Box 1209, Franklin Park, IL 60131-8209 or **Call:** (708) 455-7730 (24-hour hotline).

A SAFE AND NUTRITIOUS FORMULA

A national organization called Formula works to ensure the safety and nutritional completeness of all infant formulas. It would like to hear from parents who have had problems with infant formulas. Formula worked for the passage of the Infant Formula Act.
Write: Formula, P. O. Box 39051, Washington, DC 20016 or **Call:** (703) 527-7171.

GOOD NUTRITION FOR YOUR CHILD

Nutrition is important for the developing baby and the growing child. The Department of Health and Human Services can send you some excellent free publications to help you feed your child properly. Ask for *Good Nutrition for Your Growing Child* (FDA) 87-2218; *All About Eating for Two* (FDA) 87-2216; and *Good Nutrition for the Highchair Set* (FDA) 86-2208.
Write: Office of Public Affairs, Department of Health and Human Services, Public Health Service, Food and Drug Administration, 5600 Fishers Lane, Rockville, MD 20857.

HEALTHY FOOD CHOICES

Good health is closely related to what we eat. Making healthy food choices may reduce your risk of developing cancer and heart disease. The government can send you a pamphlet *Eating for Life* ($1.00) (118X), which offers tips on selecting good food that can help you.
Write: Consumer Information Center, Dept. 118X, Pueblo, CO 81009.

DIET, NUTRITION, AND CANCER

It is becoming apparent that what we eat relates to our chances of developing cancer. Over one third of all cancer deaths may be related to our diet and nutrition. A free booklet entitled *Diet, Nutrition and Cancer Prevention: The Good News* (513X) is available that will help you select, prepare, and serve healthier foods. A list of high-fiber and low-fat foods is included.

Write: Consumer Information Center, Dept. 513X, Pueblo, CO 81009.

A GUIDE FOR PACKING NUTRITIOUS LUNCHES

Children need well-balanced meals. Giant Food can send you a free pamphlet entitled *Bag It! A Guide To Packing Nutritious Lunches,* which gives tips on the proper selection and preparation of school lunches for children (only one free of charge). There is a fee for additional copies.

Write: Giant Food, Inc., P.O. Box 1804, D.597, Washington, DC 20013 or **Call:** (301) 341-4365.

HEALTH SNACKS

Since "grazing" is becoming the American way of eating, it is important to choose healthy snacks. The government can send you two pamphlets to help: *The Grazing of America: A Guide to Healthy Snacking and Making Bag Lunches* (516X), and *Snack, and Desserts* 115X (cost $2.50).

Write: Consumer Information Center, Dept. 516X and 115X, Pueblo, CO 81002.

A GUIDE TO QUALITY SCHOOL LUNCH AND BREAKFAST PROGRAMS

A guide for parents to evaluate and investigate lunch and breakfast programs in our schools is available. It costs $3.00.

Write: Food Research and Action Center, 1875 Connecticut Avenue, Suite 540, Washington, DC 20009 or **Call:** (202) 986-2200.

PROBLEMS WITH FOOD ADDITIVES

The Feingold Association believes that symptoms such as overactivity, A.D.D., anxiety, aggression, sleep disturbances, and learning disabilities may be associated with the intake of synthetic colors, synthetic flavors, and the preservatives, BHA, BHT, and TBHQ. It provides detailed information on how to test out the Feingold Program. The association is a nonprofit parent-support group.
Write: Feingold Association of the United States, P.O. Box 6550, Alexandria, VA 22306 or **Call:** (703) 768-FAUS.

DIET AND THE HYPERACTIVE CHILD

Evidence exists that some hyperactivity in children may be related to diet. The Feingold Program offers a technique to determine whether certain foods or food additives are contributing to the child's hyperactivity.
Write: The Feingold Association of the United States, Box 6550, Alexandria, VA 22306 or **Call:** (703) 768-FAUS; (800) 321-FAUS.

FEDERAL ASSISTANCE IN CHILD NUTRITION

Federal programs exist that can help low-income families purchase food and give instructions to mothers on proper nutrition for their children.
Write: Food Research and Action Center/National Anti-Hunger Coalition, 1875 Connecticut Avenue, Suite 540, Washington, DC 20009 or **Call:** (202) 986-2200.

> *"There is no finer investment for any community than putting milk into babies."*
>
> **Winston Churchhill, 1943**

CHILD-ADVOCATE GROUPS

A number of organizations are working at the national and local level to insure that the needs of children are met by various federal and state programs.

CHILDREN'S RIGHTS GROUP

Works with communities in expanding services to children. Offers workshops, training seminars, and technical services to parents who want to have federally funded child-nutrition programs in their neighborhood.
Write: Children's Rights Group, 543 Howard Street, San Francisco, CA 94105 or **Call:** (415) 495-7283.

CHILD WELFARE LEAGUE OF AMERICA

This organization provides consultation on matters involving child welfare services, including day care. It has an excellent collection of books, monographs, and pamphlets on a variety of issues affecting children and can send you a free catalog.
Write: Child Welfare League of America, 440 1st Street, N.W., Suite 310, Washington, DC 20001 or **Call:** (202) 638-2952.

CHILDREN'S DEFENSE FUND (CDF)

This group is involved in influencing federal and state governmental policies and legislation that relate to children. CDF can send you the latest information on pending legislation and issues affecting children. It can send you a free catalog of its publications and gifts.
Write: Children's Defense Fund, 122 C Street, N.W., Washington, DC 20001 or **Call:** (202) 628-8787.

LEGISLATION FOR CHILDREN

The Committee for Children promotes legislation that directly or indirectly benefits children, including pediatric AIDS, child care, health, safety, and environmental protection legislation as it affects children.
Write: Committee for Children, 5415 Connecticut Avenue, N.W., Suite 133, Washington, DC 20015 or **Call:** (202) 966-7396.

COURT-APPOINTED ADVOCATES FOR CHILDREN

A national organization maintains a network of programs designed to provide court-appointed special advocates for abused and neglected children involved in juvenile dependency hearings. It publishes a semiannual directory.

Write: National Court Appointed Special Advocates Association, 2722 Eastlake Avenue, E., Suite 220, Seattle, WA 98102 or **Call:** (206) 328-8588.

GRANDPARENTS'/CHILDREN'S RIGHTS

An organization concerned with the rights of emotionally, mentally, physically, and sexually abused children. It lobbies for uniform laws safeguarding the rights of children, grandparents, and grandparents' visitation rights. Acts as a clearinghouse on these subjects.

Write: Grandparents'/Children's Rights, 5728 Bayonne Avenue, Haslett, MI 48840.

DEFENSE FOR CHILDREN INTERNATIONAL

An organization which seeks to promote and protect the rights of children as defined by national and international legislation. Members are child service professionals, physicians, lawyers, and concerned individuals. Offers support in cases of child maltreatment and abuse, sexual abuse, armed conflict, forced disappearance, torture and killing, transnational kidnapping, prisons, and international slavery and prostitution.

Write: Defense for Children International - United States of America, 210 Forsyth Street, New York, NY 10002 or **Call:** (212) 353-0951.

> ***"Nature in an absolute manner wills that right should at length obtain the victory."***
>
> **Immanuel Kant**

8

HELP FOR PARENTS

A GENERAL PARENTING GUIDE Since most parents begin this honorable profession with little or no experience, some useful guidelines are welcome.

SUGGESTIONS FOR EFFECTIVE PARENTING
The Clearinghouse on Elementary and Early Childhood Education can send you a publication *Family Living* ($11.75), which contains 33 articles on parenting, young children's feelings, behavior, and learning. Also included is a resource list and computer-search reprint on parenting and family life.
Write: ERIC Clearinghouse on Elementary and Early Childhood Education, 805 W. Pennsylvania Avenue, Urbana, IL 61801.

FREE CONSUMER INFORMATION CATALOG FOR PARENTS The federal government will send you a free catalog that contains over 200 free or low-cost booklets of interest to parents. Because more than 30 federal agencies distribute some of their information through this catalog, a wide variety of topics is available, such as careers, education, child care, health, nutrition, money management, federal programs, and parenting.
Write: Consumer Information Catalog, Pueblo, CO 81009.

FREE PARENTING SEMINAR

The Lifestyle Learning Center can send you study material that addresses such issues as why children misbehave, how to deal with defiance, developing self-worth in your child, building character, teaching obedience, and negotiating with children.
Write: Parenting, Box 1000, Thousand Oaks, CA 91359.

CENTER FOR EARLY ADOLESCENCE

These people offer workshops for professionals on early adolescent development, schooling, parent education, and after-school programming. They serve as a clearinghouse for information on early adolescence.
Write: Center for Early Adolescence, Carr Mill Mall, Suite 211, University of North Carolina at Chapel Hill, Carrboro, NC 27510 or
Call: (919) 966-1148.

RESPECT FOR YOUR TEEN

The Lutheran Brotherhood has a program that helps parents help their teen surmount the challenges of youth. It can send you a free copy of the *Respecteen* booklet, "Our Families ... Our Future."
Call: (800) 888-3820.

FREE PARENTING NEWSLETTER

Family Matters is a nonprofit organization offering information and services, especially for parents. It can send you a free newsletter on parenting.
Write: Family Matters, P. O. Box 7000, Cleveland, TN 37364.

> *"Education commences at the mother's knee, and every word spoken within the hearsay of little children tends toward the formation of character."*
>
> **Hosea Ballou**

ADOPTION AND FOSTER CARE

Special people and special organizations exist to help children find parenting when it is absent in their lives.

THE NATIONAL ADOPTION CENTER

This center promotes adoption opportunities for children throughout the U.S., especially children with special needs. It operates a telecommunication network that links children waiting for adoption, adoption agencies, and prospective adoptive parents. It also provides an information and referral service and conducts public education programs.

Write: The National Adoption Center, 1218 Chestnut Street, Philadelphia, PA 19107 or **Call:** 800-TO-ADOPT; (215) 925-0200.

AID TO ADOPTION OF SPECIAL KIDS

An organization that recruits adoptive parents for children with special needs. It publicizes the need for adoptive homes for children with handicaps and other special needs.

Write: Aid to Adoption of Special Kids, 657 Mission Street, Suite 601, San Francisco, CA 94105 or **Call:** (800) 232-2751.

NATIONAL COMMITTEE FOR ADOPTION

This group works for children in need of families through its support of local member agencies and its National Adoption Hotline.

Write: National Committee for Adoption, 1930 17th Street, N.W., Washington, DC 20009-6207 or **Call:** (202) 328-1200 (will accept collect calls from pregnant women and teenagers).

NORTH AMERICAN COUNCIL ON ADOPTABLE CHILDREN

Coalition of adoptive parent groups advocating for the rights of children with physical, mental, and emotional disabilities who are waiting for permanent, continuous, nurturing families.

Write: North American Council on Adoptable Children, 1821 University Avenue, Suite N498, St. Paul, MN 55104 or **Call:** (612) 644-3036.

ORPHAN FOUNDATION

Provides guidance, support, friendship, and emergency care for children raised outside traditional family settings. Assists foster-care youth in their transition from child welfare to independent adulthood. Orphan Foundation also works with runaway children and is an advocate for the rights of abandoned children.

Write: Orphan Foundation, 1500 Massachusetts Avenue, N.W., Suite 448, Washington, DC 20005 or **Call:** (202) 861-0762.

INDEPENDENT LIVING PROGRAM

A federal program to help eligible youth make the transition from foster care to independent living. Eligible youth are those 16 and over for whom IV-E foster care maintenance payments have been made.

Write: Irene Hammond, Independent Living Program, U.S. Department of Health and Human Services, Administration for Children, Youth, and Families, Children's Bureau, Washington, DC 20201 or **Call:** (202) 245-0666.

ADOPTEE-BIRTH PARENT SUPPORT NETWORK

Can assist adoptees, adoptive parents, birth parents, siblings, attorneys, social workers, and adoption professionals with problems associated with adoption. Search assistance is provided to adoptees and birth parents who wish to locate their biological relatives.

Write: Adoptee-Birth Parent Support Network, P. O. Box 23674, L'Enfant Plaza Station, Washington, DC 20026 or **Call:** (301) 464-5755.

ADOPTION BOOKS CATALOG

Wallmark Associates can send you ($1.00) a catalog listing numerous books dealing with adoption, such as *Parenting Your Adopted Child: A Complete and Loving Guide.*

Write: Wallmark Associates, P. O. Box 173, Ringoes, NJ 08551 or **Call:** (908) 806-6695.

NATIONAL RESOURCE CENTER FOR SPECIAL NEEDS ADOPTION This division of Spaulding for Children can send you a catalog listing a variety of books and videotapes on the adoption of special children. It publishes the *Roundtable,* which informs adoption practitioners and administrators of new developments in the field of special needs adoption and shares ideas, problems, and successes. The center provides training, consultation, and technical assistance to parent groups and professionals on permanency planning, special-needs adoption, and parent adoption services.
Write: National Resource Center for Special Needs Adoption, Spaulding for Children, P. O. Box 337, Chelsea, MI 48118 or **Call:** (313) 475-8693.

ATHLETICS Sports should be a part of every young person's education. A variety of programs is involved in supporting athletics for our youth.

AAU/USA YOUTH SPORTS PROGRAM

The goal of the AAU/USA Youth Sports Program is to establish, develop, and implement a comprehensive youth-sports program for athletes 8–18. Activities in 22 sports are conducted at local, regional, and national levels.
Write: AAU/USA Youth Sports Program, 3400 W. 86th Street, P. O. Box 68207, Indianapolis, IN 46268 or **Call:** (317) 872-2900.

> *"It's not true that nice guys finish last. Nice guys are winners before the game even starts."*
>
> **Addison Walker**

AMERICAN COLLEGE OF SPORTS MEDICINE

The largest sports medicine organization in the world, with nearly 12,000 members involved in science, medicine, education, and sports. Its primary mission is to generate and disseminate research and information on the benefits and effects of exercise as well as the treatment and prevention of injuries incurred in sports, exercise, and fitness activities.

Write: American College of Sports Medicine, P.O. Box 1440, Indianapolis, IN 46206 or **Call:** (317) 637-9200.

LET'S PLAY TO GROW

A program that provides an opportunity for special children to learn through play and recreation. Free materials on how to start a *Let's Play to Grow Family Club* will be sent upon request.

Write: Let's Play to Grow, Joseph P. Kennedy, Jr., Foundation, 1350 New York Avenue, Washington, DC 20005.

SPORTS DRUG-AWARENESS PROGRAM

The Department of Justice can provide you with drug-abuse education and prevention publications that relate to sports.

Write: Drug Enforcement Administration (DEA), Demand Reduction Section, Department of Justice, Washington, DC 20537 or **Call:** (202) 307-7423.

> *"To love the game beyond the prize."*
>
> **Henry Newbolt**

GOING TO CAMP A variety of camps with different activities is available to young people. Below are two organizations that can help you make the right selections for your child.

GUIDE TO ACCREDITED CAMPS

The American Camping Association can send you a listing of over 1,800 camps, which describes their special activities, such as nutrition programs for the disadvantaged, farming, environmental education, and foreign languages. The guide costs $10.95.
Write: American Camping Association, Bradford Woods, Martinsville, IN 46151-7902 or **Call:** (317) 342-8456; (800) 428-2267.

CAMPING IN OUR NATIONAL FORESTS

The federal government can send you a brochure titled *A Guide to Your National Forests* ($1.00), which contains maps showing the locations of each national forest along with information offices to help you plan your visit.
Write: Consumer Information Center, Dept. 148X, Pueblo, CO 81009.

THE COMPUTER WORLD Computers are a big part of the world that our young people are entering. It is important that they understand how computers can help them.

HOW TO CHOOSE A COMPUTER

The purchase of a computer for your child can be an important and expensive decision. You need all the help you can get. A government pamphlet entitled *How to Buy a Personal Computer* (526X) (50¢) is a step-by-step guide to selecting a computer, floppy disks, and printer. It also contains a glossary.
Write: Consumer Information Center, Dept. 526X, Pueblo, CO 81009.

EDUCATING YOUR CHILD

The process of educating your child begins at birth. You can't leave all of your child's education to the schools. Parents play a vital role.

NATIONAL PTA

Works toward uniting the home, school, and community in behalf of children and youth. It can provide you with a number of educational materials on topics such as parent education, drug and alcohol education, latchkey children, seat belts, children's self-esteem, teen drinking and driving, and parent involvement in education.
Write: National PTA, Program Division, National Congress of Parents and Teachers, 700 Rush Street, Chicago, IL 60611 or **Call:** (312) 787-0977.

DRUG-PREVENTION CURRICULA

The Department of Education can provide you with a guide to the selection and implementation of drug-prevention curricula. It represents the best current thinking about drug-prevention education and shows what to look for when adopting ready-made curricula. Ask for the booklet *Drug Prevention Curricula.*
Write: Office of Educational Research and Improvement, U.S. Department of Education, 555 New Jersey Avenue, N.W., Washington, DC 20208-5645 or **Call:** (800) 424-1616; DC (202) 219-1651.

CLEARINGHOUSE ON ELEMENTARY AND EARLY CHILDHOOD EDUCATION

The ERIC Clearinghouse on Elementary and Early Childhood Education can provide you with a wealth of information and publications concerning all aspects of your child's early education. The ERIC database has the world's largest source of educational information. It is available to the public at more than 3,000 locations worldwide.
Write: Access ERIC, Dept. CCE, 1600 Research Blvd., Rockville, MD 20850 or **Call:** (800) USE-ERIC.

FIRST DAY AT SCHOOL

Sending a child off to school the first time can be a taxing moment for both the parent and child. The National Association for the Education of Young Children can send you a free pamphlet which will help if you will send it a self-addressed, stamped envelope. Their pamphlet, *So Many Goodbyes*, is especially helpful for parents of preschoolers.

Write: NAEYC Information Service Department, 573, 1834 Connecticut Avenue, N.W., Washington, DC 20009.

McDONALD'S EDUCATIONAL RESOURCES

McDonald's offers educational resources and films to students, their parents, and teachers on subjects which include nutrition, health and safety, drug-abuse prevention, reading, study skills, time management, career planning, and more. McDonald's has programs for all school levels. It can send you a free *Catalog of Educational Resources* describing these resources.

Write: McDonald's Education Department, McDonald's Plaza, Oak Brook, IL 60521 or **Call:** (708) 575-6198.

NATIONAL TASK FORCE ON YOUTH AT RISK

The Extension Service of the USDA operates an educational program to combat poverty, lack of family support, and negative-peer pressure for young people. It can supply you material for youth development education, parent education, and community education. Information is available on youth-at-risk activities throughout the United States.

Write: Development Information Center, USDA, National Agricultural Library, Room 304, 10301 Baltimore Blvd., Beltsville, MD 20705 or **Call:** (301) 344-3719.

ESTABLISHING DAY-CARE CENTERS

The International Child Resource Institute provides technical assistance to individuals and corporations that wish to establish and maintain day-care centers.

Write: International Child Resource Institute, 1810 Hopkins, Berkeley, CA 94707 or **Call:** (415) 644-1000.

READING AND WRITING Every child needs a foundation in the fundamentals of reading and writing. A parent's help and encouragement are needed.

PROMOTING READING

The Smithsonian Institution has a Reading Is Fundamental (RIF) Program, which promotes community projects to motivate children to read. RIF provides its projects with technical assistance, publications, an RIF film, and public service announcements promoting children's literacy. RIF is associated with the Smithsonian Institution.

Write: Reading Is Fundamental (RIF), Smithsonian Institution, 600 Maryland Avenue, S.W., Suite 500, Washington, DC 20560 or **Call:** (202) 287-3220.

READING FUNDAMENTALS FOR CHILDREN

The Department of Education has prepared a booklet *Help Your Child Become a Good Reader* (449X) (50¢) that tells you how to teach children (toddlers on up) reading fundamentals and enjoyment. Activities and suggestions center around everyday occurrences and items.

Write: Consumer Information Center, Dept. 449, Pueblo, CO 81009.

BEST BOOKS FOR CHILDREN

The Library of Congress releases a descriptive listing of the best books recently published for preschool through junior high school-age children. Ask for *Books for Children* (139X) ($1.00).

Write: Consumer Information Center, Dept. 139X, Pueblo, CO 81009.

HOW TO USE THE LIBRARY

Libraries can open up a whole new world to children. A 50¢ booklet *Helping Your Child Use the Library* (455X) discusses programs and activities for children of all ages. Includes programs for children with special needs.

Write: Consumer Information Center, Dept. 455X, Pueblo, CO 81009.

HELPING YOUR CHILD IN SCHOOL

The Department of Education has prepared a series of pamphlets (50¢ each) that give you ways to assist your child in school. They include *Help Your Child Do Better in School* (450X) (ways to improve study skills); *Help Your Child Improve in Test-Taking* (451X); *Help Your Child Learn Math* (452X); and *Help Your Child Write Well* (453X).
Write: Consumer Information Center, Pueblo, CO 81009. Send 50¢ for each pamphlet.

GRAMMAR HOTLINES

Has your child put you on the spot with one of those difficult grammar questions? Help may be only a phone call away. About 60 colleges around the country operate free grammar hotlines, with professors and graduate students to answer such questions.
Write: For a free copy of a Grammar Hotline Directory send a self-addressed, stamped, business-size-letter-envelope to Grammar Hotline Directory, Tidewater Community College Writing Center, 1700 College Crescent, Virginia Beach, VA 23456.

EDUCATING THE GIFTED CHILD

Organizations exist that can help you with the special needs of the gifted child.

GIFTED CHILD SOCIETY An organization of parents and educators interested in meeting the educational and social needs of gifted and talented students. The Gifted Child Society provides educational enrichment and support services for the gifted child, assists parents with the challenge of raising gifted children, assists educators in meeting the special needs of gifted students, and works toward public recognition and acceptance of the special needs of the gifted child.
Write: Gifted Child Society, Inc., 190 Rock Road, Glen Rock, NJ 07452 or **Call:** (201) 444-6530.

COUNCIL FOR EXCEPTIONAL CHILDREN

This organization operates a clearinghouse for information about handicapped and gifted children. It is concerned with the mentally gifted, mentally retarded, visually handicapped, auditorily handicapped, physically handicapped, and those with behavior disorders, learning disabilities, and speech defects.

Write: Council for Exceptional Children, 1920 Association Drive, Reston, VA 22091 or **Call:** (703) 620-3660.

WESTINGHOUSE SCIENCE TALENT SEARCH

Students in the last year of secondary school may enter the competition by submitting a written report on an independent research project in science, mathematics, or engineering, along with standardized test scores, transcript, and official entry form. A total of $205,000 in scholarships ranging from $40,000 to $1,000 is awarded. Deadline for entries is early December of the student's senior year in high school.

Write: Science Service, 1719 N Street, N.W., Washington, DC 20036 (for official entry form and rules) or **Call:** (202) 785-2255.

"He is best educated who is most useful."

Hubbard

EDUCATION ENHANCERS You need to encourage your child to seek out educational activities outside of school as well as in the classroom. Below are some inexpensive ways you can stretch your child's mind.

SKILLS FOR ADOLESCENCE

Lions-Quest develops and makes available comprehensive, broad-based programs and services that enable young people to gain self-confidence, good judgment, and social skills they need to cope with the challenges they face in today's world. Its main programs are Lions-Quest *Skills for Growing* (grades K-5), *Skills for Adolescents* (grades 6-8), and *Skills for Living* (grades 9-12).

Write: Quest International Headquarters, 537 Jones Road, Granville, OH 43023-0566 or **Call:** (800) 446-2700 (U.S.); (614) 522-6400 (International).

SEND YOUR CHILD INTO SPACE

NASA has a number of publications and posters to educate children about space and aerospace. One, entitled *Elementary School Aerospace Activities*, is a manual for teachers to instruct their students about the story of man and flight. *The World of Tomorrow: Aerospace Activities for 8 to 10-year-olds* presents aerospace projects children can work on.

Write: NASA Educational Publications, NASA Headquarters, Code LEP, Washington, DC 20546.

YOUR CHILD AND THE UNIVERSE

The Smithsonian Institution in Washington, DC, and a number of observatories around the country have recorded telephone messages that give the present location of the stars and planets and any unusual astronomical phenomena that may be occurring.

Call: Dial-A-Phenomenon, Smithsonian Institution, Washington, DC (202) 357-2000; Abrams Planetarium at Michigan State University (517) 332-7827; Skywatcher Report sponsored by the McDonald Observatory at the University of Texas (512) 471-5007.

LOOKING AT THE PLANETS

A $1.00 pamphlet, *A Look at the Planets* (150X), has full-color photos and describes the planets in the solar system. Includes data on space exploration.
Write: Consumer Information Center, Dept. 150X, Pueblo, CO 81009.

A GUIDE TO NORTHERN SKIES

A $1.50 booklet entitled *Stars In Your Eyes: A Guide to the Northern Skies* (155X) contains helpful hints on how to find the seven best-known constellations and an explanation of how they were named.
Write: Consumer Information Center, Dept. 155X, Pueblo, CO 81009.

A HISTORY MAGAZINE FOR YOUNG PEOPLE

If you are having difficulty interesting your child in history, a monthly magazine called *Cobblestones* should help. This magazine is dedicated toward lively and balanced reporting of what happened in the past. Over 120 back issues available.
Write: Cobblestone Publishing, Inc., 30 Grove Street, Peterborough, NH 03458.

LEARNING GEOGRAPHY

A 50¢ booklet, *Helping Your Child Learn Geography* (454X), is available that teaches your child the fundamentals of geography in a format that's challenging and fun. It includes a foldout "outline" map of the U. S. to test their newfound knowledge.
Write: Consumer Information Center, Dept. 454X, Pueblo, CO 81009.

INTRODUCE YOUR CHILD TO GARDENING

The National Gardening Association adds joy and health to living by promoting successful gardening. Its educational programs support and encourage youth gardening nationwide.
Write: Youth Gardening, National Gardening Association, 180 Flynn Avenue, Burlington, VT 05401 or **Call:** (802) 863-1308.

INSTRUCTIONS FOR OVERSEAS TRAVEL

Many of us are unfamiliar with what is required before we can travel overseas. The Department of State has prepared two pamphlets that help you make the proper arrangements. They are entitled *Your Trip Abroad* (158X) ($1.00), which gives tips on international travel, including information on passports, customs, visas, shots, and insurance; and *Foreign Entry Requirements* (459X) (50¢), which gives the visa requirements for countries and the addresses of embassies and consulates where visas may be obtained.
Write: Consumer Information Center, Dept. 158X and 459X, Pueblo, CO 81009.

INTERNATIONAL STUDENT EXCHANGE

Youth For Understanding promotes international student exchange to provide opportunities for young people to learn more about other people, languages, and cultures. It sponsors a teenage exchange program through which U.S. students can live in homes abroad and students from foreign countries can live with American families.
Write: Youth For Understanding, 3501 Newark Street, N.W., Washington, DC 20016-3167 or **Call:** (202) 966-6808; (800) TEENAGE.

SCIENCE-BY-MAIL

The Museum of Science in Boston has a program to interest your child from grades 4-6 in science. Three science-challenge packets are sent a year. Your child is hooked up with a scientist "pen pal" about solutions to the challenge. No grades. Just fun.
Write: Registrar, Science-By-Mail, Museum of Science, Science Park, Boston, MA 02114-1099 or **Call:** (800) 729-3300; (617) 589-0437.

> *"Over-optimism is waiting for your ship to come in when you haven't sent one out."*
>
> **Irv Riley**

EDUCATING THE DISADVANTAGED STUDENT

Some students have financial or social circumstances which put them at a real disadvantage in our educational system. Fortunately, a number of programs exist to help such students.

HEAD START FOR PRESCHOOLERS

The Head Start Bureau offers an array of services for low-income preschool children and their families. Included are preschool education, health education, GED- and college-credit courses for parents, and social services to resolve problems such as homelessness, substance abuse, and family violence.

Write: U.S. Department of Health and Human Services, Administration for Children, Youth and Families, Head Start Bureau, P. O. Box 1182, Washington, DC 20013.

LULAC NATIONAL EDUCATION SERVICE CENTERS

Works with disadvantaged youth to stay in school. Provides academic assistance, leadership development, college counseling, and scholarships.

Write: LULAC National Education Service Centers, 777 N. Capital Street, N.E., Suite 305, Washington, DC 20002 or **Call:** (202) 408-0060 (for information send a self-addressed, stamped envelope).

WORK FOR DISADVANTAGED YOUTH

The Training and Employment Institute helps disadvantaged youth get back into the work force and/or school. It sponsors dropout recovery and prevention programs for youth 16-21. Also provides employment training, education, and motivation.

Call: (800) 424-9103.

ARROW, INC.

American Indian Charity, founded in 1949, provides vital health care, programs preventing child/drug abuse, AIDS; supports tribal rights, law and justice.

Write: Arrow, Inc., 1000 Connecticut Avenue, N.W., Suite 1206, Washington, DC 20036.

NATIONAL COMMITTEE FOR CITIZENS IN EDUCATION An organization to help parents and citizens improve public schools for all children. NCCE provides information parents and citizens need to become involved in their local schools. It has a Spanish counselor 9 a.m. - 5 p.m. EST.

Write: National Committee for Citizens in Education, 10840 Little Patuxent Parkway, Suite 301, Columbia, MD 21044 or **Call:** (800) 638-9675 (English and Spanish).

DISADVANTAGED INNER-CITY CHILDREN

Inner-city children have a special environment and special problems. The Center for Child Protection and Family Support works toward the prevention of all forms of child maltreatment through community program development, treatment assistance, research, training, and material development. Its specific focus is on inner-city and disadvantaged children in the metropolitan Washington, DC, area.

Write: The Center for Child Protection and Family Support, 714 G Street, S.E. , Washington, DC 20003 or **Call:** (202) 544-3144.

I HAVE A DREAM FOUNDATION

An organization dedicated toward motivating "selected" grade-school students to attend college. Can supply scholarships, reading materials, support groups, and counseling.

Write: "I Have A Dream" Foundation, 330 7th Avenue, 20th Floor, New York, NY 10001 or **Call:** (212) 736-1730.

DELTA TEEN-LIFT

The Delta Sigma Theta sorority has a program to raise the aspirations of disadvantaged teenagers. An organized tour is provided to selected young people to educational, business, and cultural centers in metropolitan areas.

Write: Delta Teen-Lift, Delta Sigma Theta, Inc., 1707 New Hamphshire Avenue, N.W., Washington, DC 20009 or **Call:** (202) 483-5460.

NATIONAL BLACK CHILD DEVELOPMENT INSTITUTE Works to improve services delivered to black children and youth in child care, child welfare, health, and education both through direct services and through public education.
Write: National Black Child Development Institute, 1023 15th Street, N.W., 6th Floor, Washington, DC 20005 or **Call:** (202) 387-1281.

FINANCIAL AID FOR EDUCATION

The cost of education is skyrocketing. Fortunately, a number of programs exist to help young people with special needs.

STUDENT FINANCIAL AID
The federal government publishes a free booklet, *Student Guide –Financial Aid* (506X), that gives information about grants and loan programs for college, vocational, and technical school students.

Write: Consumer Information Center, Dept. 506X Pueblo, CO 81009.

WORK/STUDY PROGRAMS
Most colleges have programs where students can earn money while they attend. The government can send you a pamphlet, *Co-Op Education* (50¢) (473X), which explains these work/study programs. An order form is included for a listing of colleges with Co-Op programs.
Write: Consumers Information Center, Dept. 473X, Pueblo, CO 81009.

MEXICAN AMERICAN LEGAL DEFENSE AND EDUCATIONAL FUND This organization can provide counsel and assistance to Mexican Americans who qualify for legal or educational assistance.
Write: Mexican American Legal Defense and Educational Fund, 1430 K Street, N.W., #700, Washington, DC 20005 or **Call:** (202) 628-4074.

ESTABLISHING FINANCIAL INDEPENDENCE

A pamphlet has been developed by the government to help young people with their finances when they start college or are just beginning on their own. It is entitled *Getting Started: Establishing Your Financial Independence* (437V) (50¢), and gives tips on opening bank accounts, establishing credit, and choosing health and life insurance.
Write: Dept. 437V, Customer Information Center, Pueblo, CO 81009.

NATIONAL HISPANIC SCHOLARSHIP FUND

The National Hispanic Scholarship fund is an organization that provides scholarships for undergraduate and graduate students of Hispanic American background. These students must be United States citizens or permanent residents who have a Mexican American, Puerto Rican, Cuban, Caribbean, Central American, or South American heritage and who attend a college in one of the fifty states or Puerto Rico.
Write: National Hispanic Scholarship Fund, P .O. Box 728, Novato, CA 94948 or **Call:** (415) 892-9971.

UNITED NEGRO COLLEGE FUND, INC.

Scholarship funds are available to students attending one of the 41 UNCF member institutions. "A Mind is a Terrible Thing to Waste." For information contact the financial aid director at any member institution.
Write: United Negro College Fund, Inc., 500 East 62 Street, New York, NY 10021.

> *"Upon the education of the people of this country the fate of this country depends."*
>
> **Benjamin Disraeli**

LANDING A JOB The job market is a very competitive place. It pays to know what opportunities are available and how to present yourself.

INFORMATION ON TOMORROW'S JOB MARKET

The Department of Labor has prepared booklets that look at job prospects for young people entering the work force. One is entitled *Tomorrow's Jobs* (104X) ($1.00). It also points you toward other sources of information on careers, training, and financial aid. Tips on finding a job and interviewing are included. If you are interested in the requirements, prospects, and earnings for 200 occupations, ask for the bulletin *Matching Yourself With the World of Work* (102X) ($1.00).
Write: Consumer Information Center, Dept. 102X and 104X, Pueblo, CO 81009.

LANDING A GOOD JOB

A number of obstacles often stand between a young person and a good job. Among these are the ability to prepare resumes, write letters of application, and have successful interviews. A booklet is available from the Department of Labor that will really help. It is entitled *Resumes, Application Forms, Cover Letters, and Interviews* (108X) ($1.00).
Write: Consumer Information Center, Dept. 103X, Pueblo, CO 81009.

> *"There is no future in any job. The future lies in the man who holds the job."*
>
> Dr. George Crane

MILITARY SERVICE At this point we have an all-volunteer military service. Nevertheless, each young adult male must register with the Selective Service System when he becomes eighteen.

YOUR CHILD AND THE SELECTIVE SERVICE

The law requires 18-year-old males to register with the Selective Service System. All post offices have the forms. The government can send you a free booklet entitled *The Selective Service System: Information for Registrants*. It tells you what would happen if the draft were started again and how to request reclassification or postponement of induction into the armed forces.
Write: Consumer Information Center, Dept. 565X, Pueblo, CO 81009.

YOUTH ORGANIZATIONS The programs provided by youth organizations often give young people the direction and boost they need to succeed in life.

BOYS & GIRLS CLUBS OF AMERICA

Congressionally chartered, Boys & Girls Clubs of America provides services to 1200 clubs serving 1.5 million girls and boys ages 6-18 in 49 states. Clubs are located primarily in urban areas and are staffed by professionals. They conduct a variety of guidance activities every afternoon and evening. Pamphlets, manuals, guidebooks, and booklets are available.
Write: Boys & Girls Clubs of America, 771 First Avenue, New York, NY 10017 or **Call:** (212) 351-5900.

NATIONAL FFA ORGANIZATION

Fosters character development, agricultural leadership, responsible citizenship. Supplemental training opportunities are available for students preparing for careers in farming and agribusiness.
Write: National FFA Center, Box 15160, 5632 Mt. Vernon Memorial Highway, Alexandria, VA 22309 or **Call:** (703) 360-3600.

4-H PROGRAMS FOR RURAL YOUTH

A youth-education program conducted by the Cooperative Extension System and U.S. Department of Agriculture. Its purpose is to help youths in acquiring knowledge, developing life skills, and forming attitudes that will enable them to become self-directing, contributing members of society.
Write: 4-H Programs, Extension Service, U.S. Department of Agriculture, Washington, DC 20250 or **Call:** (202) 447-5853.

GIRL SCOUTS OF THE U.S.A.

Purpose is to help girls develop as happy, resourceful individuals willing to share their abilities as citizens in their homes, their communities, their country, and the world. Offers numerous programs which help girls expand their personal interests, learn new skills, and explore career possibilities.
Write: Girl Scouts of the U.S.A., 830 Third Avenue, New York, NY 10022 or **Call:** (212) 940-7500.

BOY SCOUTS OF AMERICA

Educational programs geared toward the character development, citizenship training, and mental and physical fitness of boys and young adults. Programs are offered through community-based religious, civic, and educational groups.
Write: Boy Scouts of America, 1325 Walnut Hill Lane, P.O. Box 152079, Irving, TX 75015 or **Call:** (214) 580-2000.

BIG BROTHERS/BIG SISTERS OF AMERICA

Matches at-risk youth on a ONE-TO-ONE® basis with adult volunteers who serve as mentors and role models. The school-age children are from primarily one-parent homes and are in need of additional support and guidance. Professionally trained caseworkers supervise the matches.
Write: Big Brothers/Big Sisters of America, 230 N 13th Street, Philadelphia, PA 19107 or **Call:** (215) 567-7000.

QUALITY MUSIC AND TV The music that your children listen to and the TV programs that they watch can have a major impact on their values and attitudes. Organizations exist that can alert you to undesirable music and TV for your child.

PARENT'S MUSIC RESOURCE CENTER

A nonprofit organization whose goal is to educate parents and consumers about the violent and explicit messages in popular music marketed to children. Negotiated a successful voluntary agreement with the recording industry to place consumer information on albums and tapes with lyrics related to explicit sex, violence. and explicit substance abuse. Publishes a quarterly newsletter free of charge and a video called *Rising to the Challenge* to educate parents about this issue.
Write: Parent's Music Resource Center, 1500 Arlington Boulevard, Arlington, VA 22209 or **Call:** (703) 527-9466.

PARENTS CHOICE FOUNDATION

This organization informs parents, teachers, and other child-care professionals about products and media that it believes are informative, challenging, and safe for children. Its magazine, *Parent's Choice,* provides information about movies, television, programs, books, toys and games, computer software, records, and home videocassettes.
Write: Parents Choice Foundation, P. O. Box 185, Waban, MA 02168 or **Call:** (617) 965-5913.

NATIONAL COALITION ON TELEVISION VIOLENCE

Organization dedicated to decreasing the amount of television and film violence.
Write: National Coalition on Television Violence, P.O. Box 2157, Champaign, IL 61825 or **Call:** (217) 384-1920.

USE AND ABUSE OF TV TIME

TV is a important part of many children's lives. A booklet entitled *Television and Your Family* (34-10057-2100) is available for 25¢ that focuses on wise viewing habits. It also lists other resource groups concerned with this issue.

Write: Augsburg Publishing House, 426 South Fifth Street, Box 1209, Minneapolis, MN 55440 or **Call:** (612) 330-3300.

SUPPORT FOR SINGLE PARENTS

Some single parents are at a loss when it comes to collecting unpaid child support. There are government publications and organizations that can help. Also, organizations exist to help single parents cope with their unique problems.

CHILD-SUPPORT PAYMENT HELP

The federal government will send you a free publication entitled *The Handbook on Child Support Enforcement.* This booklet tells you how to apply for child-enforcement services, find an absent parent, establish paternity, collect child support, and collect payments in another state.

Write: Customer Information Center, Dept. 552X, Pueblo, CO 81009.

NATIONAL CHILD SUPPORT ADVOCACY COALITION (NCSAC) A national umbrella for independent, grass-roots child-support advocacy organizations. It keeps an updated list of groups throughout the U.S. for referral purposes. A guide, tips, and other information are available for $3.00 plus a stamped, self-addressed envelope.

Write: National Child Support Advocacy Coalition, P.O. Box 4629, Alexandria, VA 22303-4629.

ENFORCEMENT OF CHILD SUPPORT

The Organization for the Enforcement of Child Support is a nonprofit group that educates the public and makes parents aware of their rights under present child-support laws. It conducts self-help and educational workshops. Offers educational literature and recommends and supports legislative changes. Kindly send an S.A.S. E.
Write: Organization for the Enforcement of Child Support, 119 Nicodemus Road, Reisterstown, MD 21136. Please send a S.A.S.E.

PARENTS WITHOUT PARTNERS

A self-help organization to assist separated, divorced, widowed, or never-married parents deal with their special problems. Parents Without Partners has literature, films, and book lists on single parenting for distribution. Referrals can be made to local groups and organizations that can help you.
Write: Parents Without Partners, 8807 Colesville Road, Silver Spring, MD 20910 or **Call:** (800) 637-7974 (for nonmembers interested in membership); MD (301) 588-9354.

SINGLE MOTHERS BY CHOICE

An organization primarily of professional women in their 30's and 40's who have either decided or are considering having children outside marriage. Can send you a packet of articles about single motherhood.
Write: Single Mothers By Choice, P.O. Box 1642, Gracie Square Station, New York, NY 10028 or **Call:** (212) 988-0993.

> *"When you dig another out of trouble, you find a place to bury your own."*
>
> **Anonymous**

WOMEN'S AND CHILDREN'S RIGHTS

The rights of women and children are often compromised by our society. A number of agencies are available to see that fairness prevails.

WOMEN'S LEGAL DEFENSE FUND

Ensures security and opportunity for women and their families by working for family/medical leave, employment opportunities, child-support enforcement, and elimination of family violence.
Write: Women's Legal Defense Fund, 1875 Connecticut Avenue, N.W., Suite 710, Washington, DC 20009 or **Call:** (202) 986-2600.

NATIONAL WOMEN'S LAW CENTER

NWLC champions women's rights by ensuring access and opportunities to employment, education, child and dependent care, and child-support enforcement.
Write: National Women's Law Center, 1616 P Street, N.W., Suite 100, Washington, DC 20036 or **Call:** (202) 328-5160.

THE CHILDREN'S FOUNDATION

This group addresses a number of problems caused by the feminization of poverty. It acts as a national forum for concerns of women and their children, especially child care and child support.
Write: The Children's Foundation, 725 15th Street, N.W., #505, Washington, DC 20005 or **Call:** (202) 347-3300.

> *"Believe and remember this, every saint and every sinner affects those whom he will never see, because his words and deeds stamp themselves upon the soft clay of human nature everywhere."*
>
> **Joshua Loth Liebman**

DIVORCE The trauma resulting from divorce can impact profoundly on children. Seek out help if it is needed.

JOINT CUSTODY

An organization that concerns itself with joint-custody issues and how they affect children. It surveys court decisions and their consequences and can provide you literature on this subject.
Write: Joint Custody Association, 10606 Wilkins Avenue, Los Angeles, CA 90024 or **Call:** (213) 475-5352.

CHILD'S INTEREST IN DIVORCE

The organization PACE (Parents' and Children's Equality) promotes the best interests of children in divorce and child-custody matters. It can help parents in locating and recovering children who may be victims of custodial interference or parental kidnapping.
Write: PACE, 1816 Florida Avenue, Palm Harbor, FL 34683 or **Call:** (813) 938-3063.

VOLUNTEERING Nothing enhances a young person's self-esteem more than helping others. The organization below can locate a volunteering activity that would suit your child:

PEACE CORPS

This organization can provide information to a person interested in volunteering. It can send you a brochure, *Peace Corps*, which describes various volunteering activities by people throughout the country.
Write: Peace Corps, 1990 K Street, N.W., Washington, DC 20526 or **Call:** (800) 424-8580, Ext. 2227.

9

INTERNATIONAL CHILDREN'S ORGANIZATIONS

RELIEF AGENCIES Children have problems worldwide. They are the ones who suffer the most from war, famine, and political unrest. Thanks to many compassionate international agencies, attempts are being made to ease the stress of many needy children throughout the world.

U.S. COMMITTEE FOR UNICEF

Supports United Nations Children's Fund for health, nutrition, education, and emergency relief programs throughout the developing world. UNICEF programs are thought to have saved 3 million lives in 1990 alone.
Write: U.S. Committee for UNICEF, 331 East 38th Street, New York, NY 10016 or **Call:** (800) FOR KIDS; (212) 686-5522; (800) 638-8079. .

INTERNATIONAL CHILD RESOURCE INSTITUTE

A private, nonprofit organization that promotes international exchange of information and programs concerned with children and families. It can provide technical assistance to individuals and corporations that wish to establish and improve day-care centers and family day-care homes. Publishes an International Child World Review, journals on child health, child care, and child abuse.
Write: International Child Resource Institute, 1810 Hopkins Street, Berkeley, CA 94707 or **Call:** (415) 644-1000.

PLAN INTERNATIONAL USA

Formerly Foster Parents Plan, PLAN International USA is part of a worldwide humanitarian organization linking caring sponsors with needy children and their families. PLAN combines proven, tailor-made programs with complete sponsor accountability and personal poverty. Their flagship Childreach Sponsorship program, PLAN is helping needy children and families in 26 countries of Africa, Asia, Latin America, and the Caribbean.
Write: PLAN International USA, 155 Plan Way, Dept. L024, Warwick, RI 02886 or **Call:** (800) 556-7918; (401) 738-5600.

WORLD VISION, INC.

World Vision is a Christian humanitarian organization assisting 16 million people in 80 countries through emergency relief, community development, refugee assistance, and child care.
Write: World Vision, Inc., Pasadena, CA 91131 or **Call:** (800) 423-4200.

CARE

International aid and development organization providing for self-help development, disaster aid, and health-care training overseas.
Write: CARE, 660 First Avenue, New York, NY 10016 or **Call:** (212) 686-3110.

CHILDREN'S SURVIVAL FUND

Provides medicine, milk, and food to clinics, schools, and villages worldwide. Operates disaster relief, refugee assistance, development programs to rescue children in 30 countries.
Write: Children's Survival Fund, P.O. Box 7097, Pasadena, CA 91109 or **Call:** (818) 502-1988.

HOLT INTERNATIONAL CHILDREN'S SERVICES, INC.

International adoption and child-caring agency serving homeless children in Asia and Latin America. Their motto, "Every child deserves a home of his own."
Write: Holt International Children's Services, P.O. Box 2880, Eugene, OR 97402 or **Call:** (503) 687-2202.

HELEN KELLER INTERNATIONAL

An organization that fosters blind people's independence in developing countries. This organization pioneered in using vitamin A against child blindness and promotes eye care and cataract surgery.
Write: Helen Keller International, 15 W. 16th Street, New York, NY 10011 or **Call:** (800) 638-8079; (212) 807-5800.

THE PEARL S. BUCK FOUNDATION

Assists children displaced by mixed heredity, poverty, war, hunger, homelessness, or other circumstances in Vietnam, Korea, Thailand, Taiwan, the Philippines, and Okinawa. Particular attention is given to Amerasian children who are scorned because they resemble their absent American fathers. Offers educational and medical support and psychological counseling.
Write: Pearl S. Buck Foundation, Green Hills Farm, P. O. Box 181, Perkasie, PA 18944 or **Call:** (800) 242-BUCK; (215) 249-0100.

INTERNATIONAL CHILDREN'S CARE, INC.

Cares for orphans and abandoned children worldwide.
Write: International Children's Care, Inc., 2711 N. E. 134th Street, Vancouver, WA 98686 (P.O. Box 4406, Vancouver, WA 98662) or **Call:** (800) 422-7729; (206) 573-0429.

PROJECT CONCERN INTERNATIONAL

Saves children's lives through disease prevention, improved nutrition, immunizations, and mother/child health care. Develops programs that generate self-reliance through local community participation.
Write: Project Concern International, P.O. Box 85323, San Diego, CA 92138 or **Call:** (800) 638-8079; (619) 279-9690.

SAVE THE CHILDREN

Helps impoverished children and their families in 39 countries through self-help community projects in health, nutrition, education, and economic development. Also aids victims of disaster.
Write: Save the Children, 54 Wilton Road, Westport, CT 06880 or **Call:** (800) 638-8079; (203) 226-7271.

PRESIDING BISHOP'S FUND FOR WORLD RELIEF

Relief arm of the Episcopal Church. Its purpose is to provide relief of worldwide human suffering. Responds to natural disasters and other emergencies, communicates appeals for financial aid at times of emergencies, makes grants based on four broad criteria–relief, rehabilitation, children in crises, and development.
Write: Presiding Bishop's Fund for World Relief, 815 Second Avenue, New York, NY 10017 or **Call:** (800) 334-7626; (800) 488-0087.

INTERNATIONAL SOCIAL SERVICE

Serves as a liaison between U.S. and overseas agencies to resolve problems of separated family members, emphasizing especially services to protect children. It has branches in 13 countries and cooperating agencies in well over 100.

Write: International Social Service, 95 Madison Avenue, New York, NY 10016 or **Call:** (212) 532-5858.

HEALING THE CHILDREN

An organization that helps underprivileged children in other countries have access to medical treatment in the United States. (12 chapters).

Write: Healing the Children, North 1603 Belt, Spokane, WA 99205 or **Call:** (509) 327-4281.

CHRISTIAN CHILDREN'S FUND

International, nonsectarian group which provides assistance to needy children in various countries. Sponsors are able to maintain direct contact with the child they support.

Write: Christian Children's Fund, P.O. Box 26511, Richmond, VA 23261 or **Call:** (804) 756-2700.

> *"It is a great mistake to suppose that God is only or even chiefly concerned with religion."*
>
> William Temple
> Archbishop of Canterbury

CHRISTIAN RELIEF SERVICES

Assists Native Americans, Appalachian poor, homeless, famine victims, and refugees. Provides food, clothing, medicine, water-development, housing, organic gardening on Indian reservations and economic development and youth programs to combat alcoholism and abuse. Projects are chaired by athletes Billy Mills and Mark May. Nondenominational.

Write: Christian Relief Services, 6911 Richmond Highway, Suite 300, Alexandria, VA 22306 or **Call:** (703) 765-8424.

CHURCH WORLD SERVICE/CROP

Church World Service provides emergency relief, development assistance, and aid to refugees. By working in partnership with people in more than 70 countries, CWS channels financial and materials resources to nurture long-term self-reliance. The Church World Service, U.S. network offers educational and fund-raising opportunities at the local level.

Write: Church World Service/CROP, P.O. Box 968, Elkhart, IN 46515 or **Call:** (219) 264-3102.

AMERICAN JEWISH WORLD SERVICE

International emergency relief and development agency. Its goal is to provide funding for development assistance programs in health and agriculture.

Write: American Jewish World Service, 15 W 26th Street, 9th Floor, New York, NY 10010 or **Call:** (212) 683-1161.

INTERNATIONAL LIFELINE

International Christian agency feeding malnourished indigent children. Volunteers provide medicine, child health care, immunization, surgery, community health, and family planning.

Write: International Lifeline, P.O. Box 32714, Oklahoma City, OK 73123 or **Call:** (800) 456-4464.

<u>ADVENTIST DEVELOPMENT AND RELIEF AGENCY INTERNATIONAL</u> ADRA works on behalf of parents and children in more than 70 countries worldwide. ADRA's programs stress self-reliance and concentrate on clean-water projects, growth monitoring, immunization, parent education, nutrition, hygiene, child spacing, and child care. ADRA also aids in the distribution of food to undernourished children.
Write: Adventist Development and Relief Agency, 12501 Old Columbia Pike, Silver Spring, MD 20904 or **Call:** (800) 424-ADRA; (301) 680-6380.

<u>CATHOLIC RELIEF SERVICES</u>
Overseas relief and self-help development agency of the American Catholic Community. Conducts programs of disaster response, refugee relief, and rehabilitative social welfare services, and socioeconomic development in 73 countries. Distributes food, clothing, and medicine.
Write: Catholic Relief Services, 209 W. Fayette Street, Baltimore, MD 21201-3443 **Call:** (301) 625-2220.

> *"If that thou hast the gift of strength, then know thy part is to uplift the trodden low."*
>
> **George Meredith**

THE GREATEST RESOURCE – GOD

Call: 24 hour hotline. Instant access, no telephone necessary. Children can say "Hi, God" and start talking to Him. He is always available.

I asked one of my theologian friends, Dr. Graham Maxwell, about my describing God as children's greatest resource. He replied:

"Respect for religious freedom makes us properly cautious in talking about God, especially in public schools. But children growing up in this country can hardly avoid becoming aware of some force or being called 'God.' From the humblest nickel to the pledge of allegiance they are reminded that in this nation they live under a god they can trust, and in song they ask him to bless America.

"But they also hear that hurricanes, earthquakes, and other disasters are 'acts of God.' Their history books tell of cruel wars and persecutions carried out in God's name. And if they grow up in homes that read the Bible, they know many stories of fire, flood, and destruction that seem to picture God as angry and severe. What frightened child would want to communicate with such a fearsome god?

"It should be little wonder that some children develop confusing or even forbidding conceptions of this god their nickels say we trust. And anything that seems to be the cause of hurtful stress is unavoidably a matter of concern to those for whom this book was written — people who want to help children. But their ability to help is naturally affected by their own conception of God.They could have the same god as the troubled child! Besides, is it trespassing on the children's rights to touch on this subject at all? I believe there is an understanding of God that does not jeopardize the children's freedom, but rather guarantees and reinforces it.

"At each inauguration the president solemnly places his hand on the ancient book that led the fathers of this free land to declare their trust in God. From the evidence offered in that same book I developed my personal conception of God. I see him as an infinitely powerful but equally gracious person who values nothing higher than the freedom, dignity, and individuality of his intelligent creatures, so that their love, their trust, their willingness to listen and obey may be freely given. He even prefers that we regard ourselves not as his servants but his friends.

"Of a god like this children have no need to be afraid. Moreover, to a god like this it is of supreme importance that children never be deprived of their precious ability to ask questions and make up their own minds!"

As a nurse interested in science, I have found Einstein's and Margenau's statements about the discovery of God through scientific inquiry affirming to my own understanding of God. In *The Human Side* Einstein stated, "Everyone who is seriously involved in the pursuit of science becomes convinced that a spirit is manifest in the laws of the universe, a spirit vastly superior to that of man and one in the face of which we with our modest powers must feel humble!" Dr. Henry Margenau, professor emeritus of physics at Yale, states, "If you take the top-notch scientists, you find very few atheists among them."

More than any parent I've known, God, as I know Him, loves both His good and rebellious children unconditionally. He created His children free and considers each one unique, special and irreplaceable. Love and friendship can never be commanded or forced, so God is limited in His ability to share His love and friendship with each of his children by their choice.

He invites each child to consider the evidence given about Him, in nature, in books such as the Bible, and in the lives of loving, caring people. He then permits them the freedom to make up their own minds about being friends with Him.

When children understand what God is like, they are comfortable using His 24-hour hotline anytime they want to talk with Him. God is someone they can really trust. God welcomes their questions. He delights in their uniqueness. God is their friend. God loves them. God is their greatest resource.

I would like to tell you about a very special child in my life who loved his friend God. Bill Gibson Williams, an older brother, during his brief lifetime of thirteen years filled my childhood with wonderful moments of laughter, tenderness, and love. His last gift to me was an example in courage and faith. As illness destroyed his body he bravely and loudly sang favorite songs emphasizing complete trust and faith in God whom he loved. Bill had a beautiful voice, and he kept right on singing, up to the moment his consciousness faded. I wish every child could know God as the ultimate reality, as Bill did – a reality that is worth singing about and is good.

May God's grace and peace be with you, dear reader, as you care for and help the children whose lives you touch.

MJW

APPENDIX CONTENTS

REGIONAL POISON CONTROL CENTERS

ALABAMA - Alabama Poison Center, Tuscaloosa, AL
(800) 462-0800; (205) 345-0600.

ARIZONA - Arizona Poison and Drug Information Center, Tucson, AZ
(800) 362-0101 (in state); (602) 626-6016.

CALIFORNIA - Los Angeles County Medical Association Regional Poison Control Center, Los Angeles, CA
(213) 484-5151; (800) 777-6476.

CALIFORNIA - San Francisco Bay Area Regional Poison Center, San Francisco, CA
(800) 523-2222; (415) 476-6600. They can access interpreters to help in many languages.

COLORADO - Rocky Mountain Poison Center, Denver, CO
(800) 352-3073 (in state); (303) 893-7774; (303) 629-1123 (Denver area); Montana (800) 525-5042; Wyoming (800) 442-2702.

DISTRICT OF COLUMBIA -National Capital Poison Center, Washington, DC
(202) 625-3333. (National button battery poisoning registry). May call collect in cases of button battery swallowing.

REGIONAL POISON CONTROL CENTERS (Continued)

FLORIDA - Tampa Bay Regional Poison Control Center, Tampa, FL
(800) 282-3171 (in state); (813) 253-4444.

GEORGIA - Georgia Poison Control Center, Atlanta, GA
(800) 282-5846; (404) 589-4400.

ILLINOIS - Central and Southern Illinois Poison Resource Center, Springfield, IL
(800) 252-2022; (217) 753-3330.

INDIANA - Indiana Poison Center, Indianapolis, IN
(800) 382-9097; (317) 929-2323.

IOWA - University of Iowa Hospitals and Clinics Poison Control Center, Iowa City, IA
(800) 272-6477; (319) 356-2922.

KENTUCKY - Kentucky Regional Poison Center of Kosair Children's Hospital, Louisville, KY
(800) 722-5725; (502) 589-8222.

MARYLAND - Maryland Poison Center, Baltimore, MD
(800) 492-2414 (in state); (301) 528-7701.

MICHIGAN - Poison Control Center Children's Hospital of Michigan, Detroit, MI
(313) 745-5711.

MICHIGAN - Blodgett Regional Poison Center, Grand Rapids, MI
(800) 632-2727; (616)774-7854.

MINNESOTA - Hennepin Poison Center, Minneapolis, MN
(612) 347-3141.

MINNESOTA - Minnesota Poison Control System, St. Paul, MN
(800) 222-1222; (612) 221-2113.

MISSOURI - Cardinal Glennon Children's Hospital, St. Louis, MO
(800) 366-8888; (314) 772-5200.

REGIONAL POISON CONTROL CENTERS (Continued)

NEBRASKA, IOWA, KANSAS
Midplains Poison Control Center, Omaha, NE
(800) 955-9119 (in state); (402) 390-5555. Callers from Iowa, Kansas, South Dakota, and Wyoming can reach this 800 number.

NEW JERSEY - New Jersey Poison Information and Education System, Newark, NJ
(800) 962-1253 (in state).

NEW MEXICO - New Mexico Poison and Drug Information Center, Albuquerque, NM
(800) 432-6866; (505) 843-2551.

NEW YORK - Nassau County Medical Center, Long Island Regional Poison Control Center, East Meadow, NY
(516) 542-2323.

NEW YORK - New York City Poison Center, New York, NY
(212) 764-7667; (212) 340-4494.

NORTH CAROLINA - Duke Poison Control Center, Durham, NC
(800) 672-1697; (919) 684-8111.

OHIO - Southwest Ohio Regional Poison Control System, Drug and Poison Information Center, Cincinnati, OH
(800) 872-5111 (in state); (513) 558-5111.

OHIO - Central Ohio Poison Control Center, Columbus, OH
(800) 682-7625; (614) 228-1323.

PENNSYLVANIA - Pittsburgh Poison Center, Pittsburgh, PA
(412) 681-6669.

UTAH - Regional Poison Control Center, Salt Lake City, UT
(800) 456-7707 (in state); (801) 581-2151.

WASHINGTON - Seattle Poison Center, Seattle, WA
(800)732-6985; (206) 526-2121.

STATE CHILD ABUSE & MISSING CHILDREN ORGANIZATIONS

WASHINGTON, DC
National Center for Missing and Exploited Children
(800) 843-5678; (202) 634-9836.

ALABAMA
Montgomery Area Runaway Youth Services, Montgomery
(205) 265-2652, Montgomery.

The National Children's Advocacy Center, Huntsville
(205) 533-5437, Huntsville.

ALASKA
Missing Children of America, Inc., Anchorage
(907) 248-7300, Anchorage.

Alaska Youth Advocates, Inc., Anchorage
(907) 274-6541; (907) 563-7233.

STATE ORGANIZATIONS (Continued)

CALIFORNIA

Families of Crimes of Silence (FOCOS), Hermosa Beach
(213) 372-6231.

Believe the Children – Ritualistic Abuse, Manhattan Beach
(213) 379-3514.

Thursday's Child Runaway Outreach Program, West Hills
(818) 710-1181.

Youth Development, Inc., San Diego
(619) 292-5683; (800) 448-4663.

California Child Abduction Recovery and Enforcement Council
(714) 387-8521.

Kevin Collins Foundation, San Francisco
(800) 272-0012 (out of state); Bus. (415) 771-8477 (9a.m.- 5p.m).

The Child Assault Prevention Training Center, Oakland
(510) 893-0413.

Vanished Children's Alliance, Campbell
(800) 826-4743; (408) 971-4822.

Friends of Child Find, Woodland
(916) 662-2389.

Homeless Emergency Runaway Effort, H.E.R.E., Chico
(916) 891-2794.

Identi-A-Child, Chico
(916) 895-3748.

CONNECTICUT

Friends of Child Find, Burlington
(203) 673-1500.

DISTRICT OF COLUMBIA

Sasha Bruce Youth Network
(202) 546-4900.

National Network of Runaway and Youth Services
(202) 682-4114.

STATE ORGANIZATIONS (Continued)

FLORIDA

Missing Children Center, Inc., Longwood
(407) 327-4403.

Switchboard of Miami, Inc., Miami
(305) 358-1640.

Adam Walsh Children's Resource Center, West Palm Beach
(407) 820-9000.

The Safe Harbor Runaway Center, West Palm Beach
(407) 833-2400.

Childkeyppers' International, Lake Worth
(407) 586-6695.

Children's Rights of America, Inc., Largo
(813) 587-0122.

Missing Children Help Center, Tampa
(800) 872-5437; (813) 623-5437

GEORGIA

FIND ME, Inc., La Grange
(404) 884-7419.

ILLINOIS

National Committee for the Prevention of Child Abuse, Chicago
(312) 663-3520.

Believe the Children – Ritualistic Abuse, Chicago
(708) 515-5432.

KANSAS

The Lost Child Network, Leawood
(913) 649-6723.

The Kansas Missing Children Foundation, Wichita
(316) 264-0707.

KENTUCKY

Exploited Children's Help Organization, Louisville
(502) 585-3246.

STATE ORGANIZATIONS (Continued)

MARYLAND

Missing & Exploited Children's Association, Lutherville
(301) 667-0718.

Survivors of Incest Anonymous, World Service Office, Baltimore
(301) 282-3400.

People Against Child Abuse, Inc., Annapolis
(301) 269-7816; (800) 422-3055.

MICHIGAN

Runaway Assistance Program, East Lansing
(517) 351-5757; (800) 292-4517.

National Child Safety Council, Michigan Center
(517) 764-6070.

MINNESOTA

Missing Children–Minnesota, Minneapolis
(612) 521-1188.

MISSOURI

Synergy House, Parkville
(816) 741-8700.

MONTANA

Friends of Child Find, Billings
(406) 259-6999.

Tumbleweed Runaway Program, Inc., Billings
(406) 259-2558.

NEVADA

Nevada Child Seekers, Las Vegas
(702) 796-7333.

Community, Runaway & Youth Services, Reno
(702) 323-6296.

NEW HAMPSHIRE

New Hampshire Network for Runaways and Homeless Youth
(603) 668-1920.

Friends of Child Find, Manchester
(603) 622-4457.

STATE ORGANIZATIONS (Continued)

NEW JERSEY

Search Reports, Inc., Hasbrouck Heights
(201) 288-4445.

Services for the Missing, Voorhees
(609) 693-1203.

K.I.D., Kids in Danger, Island Heights
(908) 244-3028.

NEW MEXICO

I.D. Resource Center of Albuquerque, Albuquerque
(505) 883-0983; (800) 332-2443.

Families and Youth, Inc., Las Cruces
(505) 524-7765.

NEW YORK

Cult Hotline and Clinic, New York
(212) 632-4640.

Institute for Youth Advocacy, Covenant House, New York
(212) 613-0349.

American Children Held Hostage, Inc., Brentwood
(516) 231-6240.

Children's Rights of New York, Inc., Stony Brook
(516) 751-7840.

Child Find of America, Inc., New Paltz
(800) 426-5678; Bus. (914) 255-1848.

Adam Walsh Child Resource Center, Rochester
(716) 461-1000.

Child W.A.T.C.H., Elmira
(607) 732-0562.

NORTH CAROLINA

Children's Rights of America, North Carolina, Lenoir
(704) 757-0122.

NORTH DAKOTA

Youth Works, Bismark
(701) 255-6909.

STATE ORGANIZATIONS (Continued)

OHIO

Parents of Murdered Children, Cincinnati
(513) 721-5683.

OREGON

National Missing Children's Locate Center, Gresham
(503) 665-8544; (800) 443-2751, Ext. 15;
(Sightings only) (800) 999-7846.

Hide and Seek Foundation, Salem
(503) 390-7408.

Springfield Child Abuse Resources, S.C.A.R.
(503) 746-3376.

PENNSYLVANIA

Friends of Child Find, Pittsburgh, Pennsylvania, Chapter, Pittsburgh
(412) 241-1234.

Children's Rights of Pennsylvania, Inc., Allentown
(215) 437-2971.

RHODE ISLAND

The Society for Young Victims Missing Children's Center, Newport
(401) 847-5083; (800) 999-9024.

SOUTH CAROLINA

Adam Walsh Center, Columbia
(803) 254-2326.

TEXAS

Texas Association for Stolen Children, Dallas
(214) 783-1722.

National Victim's Center, Fort Worth
(817) 877-3355.

American Association for Lost Children, Houston
(713) 466-1852; (800) 375-5683

STATE ORGANIZATIONS (Continued)

WASHINGTON

OPERATION LOOKOUT, National Center for Missing Youth
(206) 771-7335; (800) 782-7335.

Victim Witness Advocacy, Seattle Police Department
(206) 684-7777.

Family and Friends of Missing Persons & Violent Crime Victims
Homicide Survivors, (Adults and Children).
(206) 362-1081.

WISCONSIN

Friends of Child Find, Highland
(608) 929-4888.

WYOMING

Mary Ellen Rue Foundation for Missing and Exploited Children
(307) 634-8822.

Wyoming State Clearinghouse for Missing Children
(307) 777-7537.

ADDITIONS

HELP FOR CHILDREN LISTINGS BY SUBJECT

ABUSE

American Association for Protecting Children
(800) 227-5242. (Page 57).

Center on Children and The Law (American Bar Association)
(202) 331-2250. (Page 58).

Child Help, USA (counseling on child abuse)
(800) 4-A-CHILD. (Page 65).

Child Welfare League of America
(202) 638-2952. (Page 56).

Clearinghouse on Child Abuse and Neglect Information
(703) 821-2086. (Page 55).

Committee for Children
(206) 322-5050. (Page 56).

Mental Health Law Project
(202) 467-5730. (Page 58).

National Burn Victim Foundation
(201) 676-7700. (Page 58).

National Center for the Prosecution of Child Abuse
(703) 739-0321. (Page 58).

ABUSE (Continued)

National Center on Child Abuse and Neglect
(202) 245-0814. Call to find state agency. **(Page 56).**

National Child-abuse Hotline
(800) 422-4453. (Page 56).

National Committee for Prevention of Child Abuse
(312) 663-3520. (Page 57).

National Exchange Club Foundation for the Prevention of Child Abuse, The
(419) 535-3232 (Page 57).

Parents Anonymous (child abuse, over 1,200 chapters)
(800) 421-0353; CA (800) 352-0386; (213) 410-9732. (Page 59).

Parents United (Daughters & Sons; Adults Molested as Children)
(408)453-7611, Ext. 150. (Page 59).

Village of Child Help, CA.
(714) 845-3155. (Page 65).

ADOLESCENTS

Center for Early Adolescence
(919) 966-1148. (Page 140).

ADOPTION

Adoptee-Birth Parent Support Network
(301) 464-5755. (Page 142).

"ASK America," Aid to Adoption of Special Kids
(800) 232-2751. (Page 141).

National Adoption Center, The
(800) TO-ADOPT; PA (215) 925-0200. (Page 141).

National Committee for Adoption
(202) 328-1200. (Page 141).

National Resource Center for Special Needs Adoption
(313) 475-8693. (Page 143).

North American Council on Adoptable Children
(612) 644-3036. (Page 141).

AIDS

AIDS Hotline
(800) 638-6252 (Page 69).

AIDS in the Schools
(Page 70).

PHS AIDS Hotline
(800) 342-AIDS; (800) 342-2437; (800) 243-7889 (Voice/TDD); (800) 344-7432 (Spanish). (Page 69).

Terrific, Inc., Grandma's House
(202) 462-8526. (Page 70).

ALCOHOL ABUSE

Al-Anon Family Group Headquarters
(800) 356-9996; (212) 302-7240. (Page 36).

Alateen
(800) 356-9996; (212) 302-7240. (Page 36).

Alcoholics Anonymous
(212) 686-1100. (Page 35).

Alcohol Problems in Elementary School (NCADI)
(800) 729-6686: (800) SAY-NO-TO; TDD (800) 487-4889. (Page 37).

Children of Alcoholics Foundation, Inc.
(Page 36).

Coaches' Program for Drug and Alcohol Prevention
(202) 307-7936 (Page 44).

Hazelden Educational Materials
(612) 257-4010. (Page 45).

National Association for Children of Alcoholics
(714) 499-3889. (Page 36).

National Clearinghouse for Alcohol Information
(301) 468-2600; (800) 729-6686; (800) SAY-NO-TO; TDD (800) 487-4889. (Page 35, 37).

ALCOHOL ABUSE (Continued)

Suzanne Somers Institute
(Page 36).

Target-Helping Students Cope with Alcohol and Drugs
(816) 464-5400; (800) 366-6667. **(Page 37).**

Washington Regional Alcohol Programs
(301) 565-4161. **(Page 28).**

ALLERGY

American Academy of Allergy and Immunology
(800) 822-2762. **(Page 71).**

American Allergy Association
(Page 71).

ANABOLIC STEROIDS

Side Effects of Anabolic Steroids
(Page 46).

ANOREXIA

American Anorexia/Bulimia Association
(212) 734-1114. **(Page 105).**

ANAD - National Association of Anorexia Nervosa
(Anorectics and Bulimics)
(708) 831-3438. **(Page 105).**

BASH, Self-help for Anorexics and Bulimics
Crisis Hotline **(314) 768-3292; MO (800) 768-3838. BASH Information (800) 227-4785 (M–F 9 a.m.-5 p.m).** **(Page 106).**

ARTHRITIS

Arthritis Foundation
(800) 479-5044; (304) 232-5810. **(Page 72).**

ASTHMA

Asthma and Allergy Foundation of America
(800) 7-ASTHMA; (202) 466-7643. (Page 72).

National Jewish Center for Immunology and Respiratory Medicine (free care and treatment for intractable asthmatic children)
(800) 222-LUNG;(303) 355- LUNG in Denver area. **(Page 82).**

AUTISM

Autism Services Center
(304) 525-8014. (Page 108).

Autism Society of America
(301) 565-0433. (Page 108).

New York State Society for Autistic Children
(518) 459-1418. (Page 108).

AUTO RESTRAINTS

Child Auto Restraint Systems–NHTSA
(800) 424-9393; (202) 366-0123; (800) 434-9153 TTY; (202) 755-8919 TTY. (Page 25).

Family Shopping Guide -American Academy of Pediatrics
(Page 18).

BABY-SITTING

Baby-sitter Responsibilities
(Page 22).

Project Home Safe, American Home Economic Association
(800) 252-SAFE. (Page 21).

BEHAVIORAL PROBLEMS

Toughlove
(800) 333-1069; (215) 348-7090. (Page 45).

Wisconsin Clearinghouse
(800) 322-1468; (608) 263-2797. (Page 105).

BLIND/VISUALLY IMPAIRED

American Foundation for the Blind
(800) AFB-LIND; (800) 232-5463; NY (212) 620-2147(Page 118).

Blind Children's Center
(213) 664-2153 (Page 118).

Cornerstone Books (large print)
(800) 422-2546. (Page 120).

Eye Bank for Sight Restoration
(212) 980-6700. (Page 118).

Guidedog Foundation for the Blind
(800) 548-4337; (516) 265-2121. (Page 119).

Helen Keller National Center for Deaf-Blind Youths and Adults
(516) 944-8900 Voice TDD. (Page 121).

Hi-technology for the Blind
(212) 620-2171; (212) 620-2172. (Page 119).

National Association for Parents of the Visually Impaired
(800) 562-6265. (Page 120).

National Association for Visually Handicapped
(212) 889-3141; (415) 221-8753. (Page 120).

National Federation of the Blind
(301) 659-9314. (Page 119).

National Retinitis Pigmentosa Foundation
(800) 638-2300; (301) 225-9400. (Page 121).

National Society to Prevent Blindness
(800) 221-3004. (Page 121).

Recordings for the Blind
(609) 452-0606. (Page119).

BLOOD

Children's Blood Foundation
(212) 644-5790. (Page 73).

Cooley's Anemia Foundation
(800) 522-7222; NY (800) 221-3571; (212) 598-0911. (Page 73).

National Association for Sickle Cell Disease
(800) 421-8453. (Page 74).

National Hemophilia Foundation
(212) 219-8180. (Page 73).

BOOKS

Library of Congress Reading Lists for Children
(Page 148).

BREAST FEEDING

Formula (safe and nutritious)
(703) 527-7171. (Page 133).

La Leche League International
(708) 455-7730 (24 Hour Hotline). (Page 133).

Resources on Breast Feeding
(202) 625-8400. (Page 132).

BULIMIA

American Anorexia/Bulimia Association
(212) 734-1114. (Page 105).

ANAD- National Association of Anorexia Nervosa
(anorexics and bulimics)
(708) 831-3438. (Page 105).

BASH, Self-Help for Anorexics and Bulimics
(314) 768-3292; (800) 227-4785; MO (800) 768-3838. (Page 106).

BURNS

National Burn Victims Foundation
(201) 731-3112. (Page 18).

CAMPS

American Camping Association
(800) 428-2267; (317) 342-8456 (Page 145).

CANCER

American Cancer Society
(800) ACS-2345; (404) 320-3333. (Page 74).

Cancer Information Service
(800) 4-CANCER; (800)422-6237 (Page 74).

Candlelighters Childhood Cancer Foundation
(800) 366-2223; (202) 659-5136. (Page 75).

Corporate Angel Network (CAN)
(914) 328-1313. (Page75).

Diet, Nutrition, and Cancer
(Page 134).

Leukemia Society of America
(703) 960-1100 (may call collect) **(Page 75).**

Skin Cancer Foundation
(212) 725-5176. (Page 89).

CAREER

Information on Tomorrow's Job Market
(Page 158).

National Future Farmers of America Organization
(703) 360-3600. (Page 159).

CEREBRAL PALSY

United Cerebral Palsy Association
(800) USA-1UCP; (212) 268-6655; (212) 481-6342. (Page 84).

CHILD ADVOCATES

Children's Defense Fund
(202) 628-8787. (Page 136).

Children's Rights Group
(415) 495-7283. Page (136).

Child Welfare League of America
(202) 638-2952. Page (56).

Committee for Children
(202) 966-7396; (Page 136).

Defense for Children International - United States of America
(212) 353-0951 (Page 137).

Grandparents'/Children's Rights
(Page 137).

National Court Appointed Special Advocates Association
(206) 328-8588. (Page 137).

CHILD CARE

Healthy Mothers, Healthy Babies
(202) 863-2458. (Page 131).

Multiple Births
(312) 266-9093. (Page 131).

National Center for Education in Maternal and Child Health
(202) 625-8410. (Page 130).

National Maternal and Child Health Clearinghouse
(202) 625-8410. (Page 129).

CHILD SUPPORT

Children's Foundation, The
(202) 347-3300. (Page 164).

Child Support Payment Help
(Page 162).

National Child Support Advocacy Coalition
(Page 162).

National Woman's Law Center
(202) 328-5160. (Page 164).

Organization for the Enforcement of Child Support
(Page 163).

Women's Legal Defense Fund
(202) 986-2600. (Page 164).

CLEFT PALATE

Cleft Palate Foundation
(800) 24-CLEFT; PA (800) 23-CLEFT (Page 115).

CLOTHES FOR SPECIAL CHILDREN

Projects for Special Children
(703) 549-2640. (Page 117).

Special Clothes for Special Children
(703) 683-7343. (Page 117).

COCAINE

Confidential Cocaine Referral Line
(800) 662-HELP. (Page 38).

National Cocaine Helpline
(800) COC-AINE. (Page 39).

COMPUTERS

How to Choose a Computer
(Page 145).

CONSUMER PRODUCT SAFETY

Consumer Product Safety Commission
(800) 638-2772; (800) 638-CPSC; (800) 638-8270 TTY. (Page 17).

CONTRACEPTIVES

Contraceptive information
(Page 50).

CREATIVE CHILDREN

Council for Exceptional Children
(703) 620-3660. (Page 150).

Gifted Child Society
(201) 444-6530. (Page 149).

CRIBS

Safe Cribs
(800) 638-2772. (Page 17).

CRIPPLED CHILDREN

National Easter Seal Society for Crippled Children and Adults
(312) 726-6200 (Page 114).

National Foundation - March of Dimes
(914) 997-4636 (Page 114).

CULTS

American Family Foundation
(212) 249-7693. (Page 30).

Cult Awareness Network
(312) 267-7777. (Page 30).

CYSTIC FIBROSIS

Cystic Fibrosis Foundation
(800) FIGHT CF; (301) 951-4422. (Page 76).

DEAF/BLIND

Helen Keller National Center for Deaf-Blind Youths & Adults
(516) 944-8900 (Voice/TDD). (Page 121).

DEAF/HEARING IMPAIRED

Alexander Graham Bell Association for the Deaf
(202) 337-5220. (Page 122).

American Society for Deaf Children
(301) 585-5400 (Voice/TDD) (PAGE 122).

Assessment Center for Hearing Impaired Children and Youth
(202) 651-5337; (202) 651-5031 (Voice/TDD). (Page 125).

Deafpride, Inc.
(202) 675-6700 (Voice/TTY). (Page 122).

Educating a Hearing Impaired Child, TRIPOD Grapevine
(800) 352-8888; CA (800) 2-TRIPOD. (Page 126).

Genetic Service Center (for the deaf)
(800) 451-8834, Ext. 5258 (Voice/TTD); (202) 651-5258. (Page 125).

Helen Keller National Center for Deaf-Blind Youths
(516) 944-8900 (Voice/TDD). (Page 121).

International Hearing Dogs
(303) 287-3277. (Page 124).

International Organization for the Education of the Hearing-impaired
(202) 337-5220. (Page 126).

Modern Talking Picture Service
(800) 237-6213 (Voice/TTY; (813) 545-8781 (Voice/TTY). (Page 123).

National Captioning Institute
(703) 998-2400 (Voice/TTY). (Page 124).

Parents of Deaf Children (Alexander Gram Bell Assoc. for the Deaf)
(202) 337-5220. (Page 122).

Parents of Hearing-impaired Children
(202) 337-5220. (Page 126).

Project: Second Chance (Deafpride)
(202) 675-6700 (Voice/TTY). (Page 123).

Registry of Interpreters for the Deaf
(301) 608-0050 (Voice/TTY). (Page 124).

Special Needs Project
(805) 565-1914. (Page 127).

DEATH

Children's Hospice International
(800) 24 CHILD; (703) 684-0330. (Page 99).

Compassionate Friends, The
(708) 990-0010. (Page 96).

Parents of Murdered Children
(513) 721-5683. (Page 33).

DIABETES

American Diabetes Association
(212) 947-9707. (Page 76).

Diabetes Research Institute Foundation
(800) 321-3437; (305) 477-3437. (Page 77).

Joslin Diabetes Center
(617) 732-2400. (Page 76).

DIGESTIVE DISORDERS

Crohns & Colitis Foundation of America
(800) 343-3637; (212) 685-3440. Page 77).

Gluten Intolerance Group
(206) 325-6980. (Page 78).

National Registry for MPS/ML Disorders
(312) 407-4007. (Page 78).

DISASTER

Coping With a Flood
(Page 19).

Coping With an Earthquake
(Page 19).

In Time of Emergency, Federal Emergency Management Agency
(Page 19).

DIVORCE

Joint Custody Association
(213) 475-5352. (Page 165).

Parents' and Children's Equality (PACE)
(813) 938-3063. (Page 165).

DOWN SYNDROME

National Down Syndrome Congress
(800) 232-6372; (708) 823-7550. (Page 109).

National Down Syndrome Society
(800) 221-4602. (Page 109).

Parents of Down Syndrome Children
(301) 984-5792. (Page 109).

DRUGS

American Council for Drug Education
(301) 294-0600. (Page 39).

C. E. Mendez Foundation
(813) 251-3600. (Page 41).

Captain Crimefighter's Drugbuster Program
(904) 343-2101. (Page 54).

Coaches' Program for Drug and Alcohol Prevention
(202) 307-7936. (Page 44).

Cocaine Helpline
(800) COCAINE. (Page 39).

Committees of Correspondence
(508) 774-2641. (Page 39).

Community Intervention Inc.
(800) 328-0417; (612) 332-6537. (Page 42).

Confidential Cocaine Referral Line
(800) 662-HELP. (Page 38).

Drug Education Information
(202) 633-1469. (Page 44).

Drug Enforcement Administration (Department of Justice)
(202) 633-1469. (Page 44).

Drug-free Schools Recognition Program (Department of Education)
(202) 219-2134. (Page 43).

Drug-Prevention Curricula
(202) 219-1651. (Page 146).

Hazelden Foundation
(612) 257-4010. (Page 45).

Just Say No Foundation
(800) 258-2766; (415) 939-6666. (Page 44).

Nar-anon Family Group
(213) 547-5800. (Page 45).

Narcotics Education, Inc.
(800) 548-8700; (301) 790-9735. (Page 38).

DRUGS (Continued)

National Clearinghouse for Drug Abuse and Alcohol
(800) 662-HELP; (800) 729-6686; (301) 468-2600. (Page 38)

National Families in Action
(404) 934-6364. (Page 41).

National Parent's Resources Institute for Drug Education
(404) 577-4500. (Page 40).

NFP REACH America
(505) 345-7134. (Page 41).

Parents for Drug-free Youth (National Federation of Parents)
(314) 968-1322. (Page 40).

Programs for Indian Youth
(202) 219-1129. (Page 42).

Programs for Native Hawaiians
(808) 842-5802. (Page 41).

Sports Drug-awareness Program
(202) 307-7423. (Page 144).

Straight, Inc.
(813) 576-8929. (Page 45).

Veterans Against Drugs
(703) 519-7009; (800) 487-1970. (Page 42).

Youth to Youth
(614) 224-4506. (Page 44).

DRUNK DRIVERS

MADD (Mothers Against Drunk Driving)
(800) GET MADD; (214) 744-6233 (Page 28).

RID (Remove Intoxicated Drivers)
(518) 327-0034. (Page 28).

SADD (Students Against Driving Drunk)
(508) 481-3568. (Page 27).

DWARFS

Little People of America
(301) 589-0730. (Page 115).

Little People Research Fund
(301) 494-0055; (800) 232-LPRF. (Page 115).

DYSLEXIA

Orton Dyslexia Society
(800) 222-2123; (301) 296-0232. (Page 84).

EATING DISORDERS

American Anorexia/Bulimia Association
(212) 734-1114. (Page 105).

BASH, Self-help for Anorexics and Bulimics
(314) 768-3292; MO (800) 768-3838; Bash Info. (800) 227-4785. (Page 106).

National Association of Anorexia Nervosa and Associated Disorders
(708) 831-3438. (Page 105).

Overeaters Anonymous
(213) 618-8835. (Page 106).

EDUCATING THE DISABLED

Center for Special Education Technology
(800) 873-8255; (703) 620-3660. (Page 117).

National Information for Children and Youth with Disabilities
(703) 893-6061; (800) 999-5599; (703) 893-8614. (Page 111).

EDUCATING THE DISADVANTAGED

Arrow, Inc.
(Page 154).

Center for Child Protection and Family Support
(202) 544-3144. (Page 155).

Delta Teen-Lift
(202) 483-5460. (Page 155).

Head Start for Preschoolers
(Page 154).

I Have a Dream Foundation
(212) 736-1730. (Page 155).

LULAC National Education Service Centers
(202) 408-0060. (Page 154).

National Black Child Development Institute
(202) 387-1281. (Page 156).

National Committee for Citizens in Education
(800) 638-9675. (Page 155).

Training and Employment Institute
(800) 424-9103. (Page 154).

EDUCATING THE GIFTED

Council for Exceptional Children
(703) 620-3660. (Page 150).

Gifted Child Society, Inc.
(201) 444-6530. (Page 149).

Westinghouse Science Talent Search
(202) 785-2255. (Page 150).

Your Child and the Universe (Observatories)
(202) 357-20000; (517) 332-7827; (512) 471-5007. (Page 151).

United States Department of Education
(202) 219-1651; (800) 424-1616. (Page 146).

EDUCATION

Clearinghouse on Elementary and Early Childhood Education
(800) USE-ERIC. (Page 146).

Development Information Center (USDA)
(301) 344-3719. (Page 147).

Establishing Day-care Centers
(415) 644-1000. (Page 147).

Grammar Hotlines
(Page 149).

Helping Your Child In School
(Page 149).

International Child Resource Institute
(415) 644-1000. (Page 168).

McDonald's Catalog of Educational Resources
(708) 575-6198. (Page 147).

National Association for the Education of Young Children
(Page 147).

National PTA
(312) 787-0977. (Page 146).

Tidewater Community College Writing Center
(Page 149).

U.S. Department of Agriculture Development Information Center
(301) 344-3719. (Page 147).

United States Department of Education
(202) 219-1651; (800) 424-1616. (Page 146).

EDUCATION ENHANCERS

Cobblestone Publishing, Inc.
(Page 152)

Instructions for Overseas Travel
(Page 153).

EDUCATION ENHANCERS (Continued)

Introduce Your Child to Gardening
(802) 863-1308. (Page 152).

Quest International Headquarters
International (614) 522-6400; (800) 446-2700. (Page 151).

Science-by-Mail
(800) 729-3300; (617) 589-0437. (Page 153).

Send Your Child Into Space
(Page 151).

Westinghouse Science Talent Search
(202) 785-2255. (Page 150).

Your Child and the Universe (Observatories)
(202) 357-20000; (517) 332-7827; (512) 471-5007. (Page 151).

Youth for Understanding
(800) TEENAGE; (202) 966-6808 (Page 153).

EMERGENCY

Federal Emergency Management Agency
(Page 19).

EPILEPSY

Epilepsy Foundation of America
(800) 332-1000; (301) 459-3700. (Page 83).

EYE

Eye Bank for Sight Restoration
(212) 980-6700. (Page 118).

National Retinitis Pigmentosa Foundation
(800) 638-2300; (301) 225-9400. (Page 121).

FINANCIAL AID

Establishing Financial Independence
(Page 157).

Mexican American Legal Defense and Education Fund
(202) 628-4074. (Page 156).

National Hispanic Scholarship Fund
(415) 892-9971. (Page 157).

Student Financial Aid
(Page 156).

United Negro College Fund
(Page 157).

FIRE

National Burn Victim Foundation
(201) 731-3112. (Page 18)

National Fire Safety Council
(517) 764-2811. (Page 18).

GARDENING

Introduce Your Child to Gardening
(802) 863-1308. (Page 152).

GENETIC SERVICES

Genetic Services Center for the Deaf
(800) 451-8834, Ext. 5258; (202) 651-5258. (Page 125).

GIFTED-CREATIVE CHILDREN

Council for Exceptional Children
(703) 620-3660. (Page 150).

Gifted Child Society
(201) 444-6530. (Page 149).

HANDICAPPED

Center for Persons With Disabilities
(801) 750-1981. (Page 112).

Center for Special Education Technology
(800) 873-8255; (703) 620-3660. (Page 117).

Clearinghouse for Disability Information
(202) 732-1245. (Page 112).

Hotline for Children and Youth With Disabilities
(800) 999-5599; (703) 893-6061. (Page 111).

National Information for Children and Youth with Handicaps
(703) 893-6061; (800) 999-5599; (703) 893-8614. (Page 111).

Projects for Special Children
(703) 549-2640. (Page 117).

Sibling Information Network
(203) 282-7050. (Page 113).

Special Clothes for Special Children
(703) 683-7343. (Page 117).

Toys for Special Children
(914) 478-0960. (Page 117).

HEALTH

Association for the Care of Children's Health
(301) 654-6549. (Page 68)

Department of Health and Human Services
(301) 496-5133. (Page 68).

Directory of Health Services
(301) 443-2086 (Page 68).

National Center for Clinical Infant Program
(703) 528-4300. (Page 68).

National Health Information Center
(800) 336-4797. (Page 67).

National Institute of Child Health and Human Development
(301) 496-5133. (Page 68).

HEART

American Heart Association
(214) 706-1179. (Page 78).

HEMOPHILIA

National Hemophilia Foundation
(212) 219-8180. (Page 73).

HOSPITALS

Children in Hospitals
(508) 369-4467. (Page 95).

City of Hope/Cancer and Major Diseases Center
(800) 423-7119. (Page 99).

Federal Hill-Burton Free Care Program
(800) 638-0742; MD (800) 492-0359. (Page 100).

Holiday Project, The
(212) 532-6158). (Page 95).

Johns Hopkins Children's Center
(301) 955-2000. (Page 97).

Little City for Retarded Children
(312) 282-2207. (Page 99).

National Jewish Center for Immunology and Respiratory Medicine
(800) 222-LUNG. (Page 98).

NIH Studies (free medical)
(301) 496-4891. (Page 99).

St. Jude Children's Research Hospital
(901) 522-0300. (Page 97).

Sammy Davis Jr. National Liver Institute
(201) 456-4535. (Page 98).

Shriner's Hospital for Children (free orthopedic and burn treatment).
(800) 237-5055; FL (800) 282-9161. (Page 98).

ILL CHILDREN

Famous Fone Friends
(213) 204-5683. (Page 95).

Holiday Project, The
(212) 532-6158. (Page 95).

Laughter Therapy
(408) 625-3788. (Page 95).

Pediatric Projects, Inc.
(818) 705-3660. (Page 96).

IMMUNIZATION

Guide to Childhood Immunization
(Page 79).

National Vaccine Information Center
(703) 938-3783. (Page 79).

INJURY

Brain-injured Children
(612) 521-2266. (Page 80).

Freedom of Information Office, CPS
(301) 492-5785. (Page 22).

Injury Information Clearinghouse
(301) 492-6424. (Page 22).

National Head Injury Foundation, The
(800) 444-NHIF (families of injured only); (202) 296-NHIF (Page 25, 80).

National Spinal Cord Injury Association
(800) 962-9629. (Page 81).

Safety Publications
(Page 23).

INTERNATIONAL ORGANIZATIONS

Adventist Development and Relief Agency
(800) 424-ADRA; (301) 680-6380. (Page 173).

American Jewish World Service
(212) 683-1161. (Page 172).

CARE
(212) 686-3110. (Page 168).

Catholic Relief Services
(301) 625-2220. (Page 173).

Children's Survival Fund
(818) 502-1988. (Page 169).

Christian Children's Fund
(804) 756-2700. (Page 171).

Christian Relief Services
(703) 765-8424. (Page 172).

Church World Service/CROP
(219) 264-3102. (Page 172).

Healing the Children
(509) 327-4281. (Page 171).

Helen Keller International
(800) 638-8079; (212) 807-5800. (Page 169).

Holt International Children's Services
(503) 687-2202. (Page 169).

International Child Resource Institute
(415) 644-1000. (Page 168).

International Children's Care, Inc.
(800) 422-7729; (206) 573-0429. (Page 170).

International Lifeline
(800) 456-4464. (Page 172).

International Social Service
(212) 532-5858. (Page 171).

INTERNATIONAL ORGANIZATIONS (Continued)

Pearl S. Buck Foundation
(800)242-BUCK; (215) 249-0100. (Page 169).

PLAN International U.S.A.
(800) 556-7918; (401) 738-5600. (Page 168).

Presiding Bishop's Fund for World Relief
(800) 334-7626; (800) 488-0087. (Page 170).

Project Concern International
(800) 638-8079; (619) 279-9690. (Page 170).

Save the Children
(800) 638-80790; (203) 226-7271. (Page 170).

U. S. Committee for UNICEF
(800) 638-8079; (212) 686-5522. (Page 167).

World Vision
(800) 423-4200. (Page 168).

JOBS

Job Outlook for the Future
(Page 158).

Landing a Good Job
(Page 158)

Peace Corps
(800) 424-8580, Ext. 2227. (Page 165).

KIDNEY

American Kidney Fund
(800) 638-8299. (Page 81).

National Kidney Foundation
(800) 622-9010; (212) 889-2210. (Page 81).

LATCHKEY CHILDREN

American Association of University Women (Phonefriend)
(814) 234-9036. (Page 21).

Project Home Safe
(800) 252-SAFE. (Page 21).

Project Latchkey, National PTA
(312) 787-0977. (Page 21).

LAUGHTER THERAPY

Old Candid Camera Tapes for Patients
(408) 625-3788. (Page 95).

LEAD POISONING

Preventing lead poisoning
(Page 20).

LEUKEMIA

Leukemia Society of America
(703) 960-1100 (Page 75).

LIVER

American Liver Foundation
(201) 256-2550. (Page 82).

Children's Liver Foundation
(818) 906-3021. (Page 82).

Sammy Davis, Jr., National Liver Institute
(201) 456-4535; (201) 456-7291. (Page 98).

LUNG

American Lung Association
(212) 315-8700. (Page 82).

Lung Line
(800) 222-LUNG. (Page 82).

MATERNAL & CHILD CARE

Directory of Organizations Related to Maternal and Child Care
(202) 625-8410. (Page 129).

Effects of Alcohol on Pregnancy
(301) 468-2600. (Page 130).

Healthy Mothers, Healthy Babies
(202) 863-2458. (Page 131).

Hotlines for Baby Nutrition and Care **(Page 132).**

Beech-Nut Nutrition Hotline
(800) 523-6633.

Gerber Products Co.
(800) 443-7237.

Johnson & Johnson Baby Products Information Center
(800) 526-3967.

Multiple Births
(312) 266-9093. (Page 131).

National Center for Education in Maternal and Child Health
(202) 625-8400. (Page 130).

National Maternal and Child Health Clearinghouse
(202) 625-8410. (Page 129)

Pregnancy After 35
(301) 496-5133. (Page 131).

Pregnancy and Infant Loss Center
(612) 473-9372. (Page 132).

MEDICAL CARE (FREE)

Free or Low-cost Medical Care
Hotline (800) 638-0742 (MD); (800) 492-0359 (Page 100).

Lung Line
(800) 222-LUNG; (303) 355-LUNG. (Page 82).

MENTAL HEALTH

Children with Attention-Deficit Disorders
(305) 587-3700. (Page 104).

Creative Therapeutics
(800) 544-6162; (201) 567-7295. (Page 104).

Dealing With Phobias and Panic
(Page 103).

Federation of Families for Children's Mental Health
(703) 684-7710. (Page 102).

Guide to Mental Health Services
(Page 102).

Mental Health Tapes
(Page 103).

National Alliance for the Mentally Ill
(703) 524-7600. (Page 102).

National Clearinghouse of Mental Health Information
(301) 443-4513; (301) 443-4514. (Page 101).

National Foundation for Depressive Illness
(800) 248-4344. (Page 103).

National Self-Help Clearinghouse
(212) 642-2944. (Page 102).

Questions on Schizophrenia
(Page 104).

MENTAL HEALTH (Continued)

What to Do When a Friend Is Depressed
(301) 443-4513. (Page 104).

Wisconsin Clearinghouse
(800) 322-1468; (608) 263-2797. (Page 105).

MENTAL RETARDATION

American Association on Mental Retardation
(202) 387-1968. (Page 107).

Association for Retarded Citizens of the U.S.
(817) 261-6033. (Page 107).

Special Olympics International
(202) 628-3630. (Page 107).

MISSING CHILDREN

Adam Walsh Child Resource Centers
(800) 843-5678; SC(803) 254-2326; NY(716) 461-1000; (716) 244-8920; CA(714) 898-4802; FL(407) 820-9000. (Page 65).

Child Find of America, Inc.
(800) I-AM-LOST; (800) A-WAY-OUT. (Page 61).

Child Keyppers' International
(407) 586-6695. (Page 62).

Children's Rights of America
(800) 442-HOPE; (813) 587-0122. (Page 63).

Exploited Children's Help Organization
(502) 585-3246. (Page 61).

Hotline for Missing and Exploited Children
(800) 843-5678. (Page 60).

Missing Children Help Center
(800) USA-KIDS; (813) 623-KIDS (Page 62).

National Center for Missing and Exploited Children
(800) 843-5678; VA (703) 235-3900. (Page 60).

National Child Safety Council, Missing Children's Division
(800) 222-1464; (517) 764-6070. (Page 62).

National Missing Children Locate Center
(503) 665-8544; (800) 443-2751, Ext. 15, (out of state); (800) 999-7846, (sightings only). (Page 63).

Operation Lookout
(800) 782-SEEK; (206) 771-7335. (Page 60).

State Department, International Child Abduction, The
(202) 647-3666. (Page 63).

Vanished Children's Alliance
(800) 826-4743; (408) 971-4822. (Page 61).

MULTIPLE SCLEROSIS

National Multiple Sclerosis Society
(800) 624-8236; (212) 986-3240. (Page 83).

MURDERED CHILDREN

Parents Who Have Experienced the Tragedy of a Murdered Child
(513) 721-5683. (Page 33).

MUSCULAR DYSTROPHY

Muscular Dystrophy Association
(800) 223-6666; (602) 529-2000. (Page 83).

MUSIC

Parent's Music Resource Center (rating system)
(703) 527-9466. (Page 161).

NARCOLEPSY

American Narcolepsy Association
(415) 788-4793. (Page 84).

NICOTINE ADDICTION

How to Stop Smoking
(Page 46).

Public Health Service Technical Information Center
(301) 443-1690. (Page 46).

NUTRITION

Beech-Nut Nutrition Hotline
(800) 523-6633. (Page 132).

Diet, Nutrition, and Cancer
(Page 134).

Federal Assistance in Child Nutrition
(202) 986-2200 (Page 135).

Feingold Association of the United States
(703) 768-FAUS; (800) 321-FAUS. (Page 135).

Food Research and Action Center
(202) 986-2200. (Page 134, 135).

Formula
(703) 527-7171. (Page 133).

Gerber Products Company
(800) 443-7237. (Page 132).

Giant Food, Inc
(301) 341-4365. (Page 134).

Good Nutrition for Your Child
(Page 133).

Guide for Packing Nutritious Lunches, A
(301) 341-4365. (Page 134).

Guide to Quality School Lunch and Breakfast Programs, A
(Page 134).

Johnson & Johnson Baby Products Information Center
(800) 526-3967. (Page 132).

OBESITY

Childhood Obesity
(301) 496-5133. (Page 106).

OBSERVATORIES

Abrams Planetarium at Michigan State University
(517) 332-7827. (Page 151).

Dial-A-Phenomenon, Smithsonian Institution, Washington, DC.
(202) 357-2000. (Page 151).

Skywatchers Report, University of Texas
(512) 471-5007. (Page 151).

ORGANIZATIONS (YOUTH)

Big Brothers/Big Sisters of America
(215) 567-7000. (Page 160).

Boy Scouts of America
(214) 580-2000. (Page 160).

Boys & Girls Clubs of America
(212) 351-5900. (Page 159).

4-H Programs for Rural Youth
(202) 447-5853. (Page 160).

Girl Scouts of the U.S.A.
(212) 940-7500. (Page 160).

National Future Farmers of America Organization
(703) 360-3600. (Page 159).

ORPHAN

Orphan Foundation
(202) 861-0762. (Page 142).

OUTDOOR SAFETY

Federal Emergency Management Agency
(Page 19).

Hug-A-Tree and Survive
(Page 19).

PARALYSIS

American Paralysis Association
(800) 526-3456; (800) 225-0292. (Page 84).

PARENTAL ASSISTANCE

Center for Early Adolescence
(919) 966-1148. (Page 140).

Child-support Payment Help
(Page 162).

Free Consumer Information Catalog
(Page 139).

Free Parenting Seminar
(Page 140).

Parents Choice Foundation
(617) 965-5913. (Page 161).

Parents Without Partners
(800) 637-7974; (301) 588-9354. (Page 163).

Single Mothers by Choice
(212) 988-0993. (Page 163).

Use and Abuse of TV Time
(612) 330-3300. (Page 162).

PEDESTRIAN SAFETY

National Highways Safety Administration, NTS-23
(202) 366-2696. (Page 26).

PEDIATRICS

American Academy of Pediatrics
(Page 18).

PESTICIDE

National Pesticide Telecommunications Network
(800) 858-7378. (Page 20).

PHOBIA

Phobia Society of America
(Page 103).

PHYSICALLY IMPAIRED

Association for Persons With Severe Handicaps
(206) 523-8446. (Page 114).

National Easter Seal Society for Crippled Children and Adults
(312) 726-6200. (Page 114).

National Foundation - March of Dimes
(914) 997-4636. (Page 114).

National Handicapped Sports
(301) 652-7505. (Page 113).

PHYSICALLY IMPAIRED (Continued)

School Reintegration Program
(714) 824-0800, Ext. 6555. (Page 114).

Special Recreation, Inc.
(319) 337-7578. (Page 113).

POISONING (FOOD)

Food and Drug Administration, Office of Consumer Affairs
(Page 24).

Food Poisoning Pamphlet
(Page 24).

PORNOGRAPHY

Child Pornography Tipline
(800) 843-5678; TDD (800) 826-7653. (Page 64).

Children of the Night
(800) 564-COTN; (818) 908-4470. (Page 48).

National Coalition Against Pornography
(513) 521-6227. (Page 64).

PREGNANCY

Adolescent Pregnancy Prevention Clearinghouse
(202) 628-8787. (Page 49).

Adolescent Pregnancy Program
(301) 585-6636; (202) 245-7473. (Page 49).

American College of Obstetricians and Gynecologists
(Page 49).

Breast-feeding
(202) 625-8400. (Page 132).

Healthy Mothers, Healthy Babies
(202) 863-2458. (Page 131).

LaMaze Childbirth
(800) 368-4404; (202) 857-1128. (Page 131).

Multiple Births
(312) 266-9093. (Page 131).

National Clearinghouse for Alcohol Information, Pregnancy
(301) 468-2600. (Page 130).

Pregnancy After 35
(301) 496-5133. (Page 131).

Pregnancy and Infant Loss Center
(612) 473-9372. (Page 132).

Teens-Helping-Teens Phone Line
(919) 774-9515. (Page 50).

RADON

Environmental Protection Agency/Radon Division
(800) SOS-RADON. (Page 20).

RAPE

King County Sexual Assault Resource Center
(206) 226-RAPE; (206) 226-5062. (Page 52).

Rape Prevention and Treatment Resources
(Page 52).

Women Against Rape (W.A.R.)
(609) 858-7800. (Page 52).

RARE DISORDERS

Cornelia De Lange Syndrome Foundation
(800) 223-8355; (203) 693-0159. (Page 87).

International Rett Syndrome Association
(301) 248-7031. (Page 87).

National Ataxia Foundation
(612) 473-7666. (Page 86).

National Hydrocephalus Foundation
(815) 467-6548. (Page 87).

National Neurofibromatosis Foundation
(800) 323-7938; NY (212) 460-8980. (Page 90).

National Organization for Albinism and Hypopigmentation
(215) 545-2322; (800) 473-2310. (Page 86).

National Organization for Rare Disorders
(800) 999-6673. (Page 86).

National Tay-Sachs and Allied Diseases Association
(617) 277-4463. (Page 87).

Scleroderma Federation
(212) 427-7040. (Page 86).

Tourette Syndrome Association
(800) 237-0717; (718) 224-2999. (Page 88).

Tuberous Sclerosis Association, Inc.
(800) 225-6872; (301) 459-9888. (Page 88).

READING

Best Books for Children
(Page 148).

McDonald's Catalog of Educational Resources
(312) 575-6198. (Page 147).

Smithsonian Reading Is Fundamental (RIF)
(202) 287-3220. (Page 148).

REYE'S SYNDROME

National Reye's Syndrome Foundation
(800) 233-7393; OHIO (800) 231-7393. (Page 88).

RUNAWAYS

Children of the Night (pornography and prostitution)
(818) 908-4470; CA (800) 564-COTN (Page 48).

Covenant House
(800) 999-9999; (212) 330-0469. (Page 48).

Directory of Runaway Programs
(202) 245-0102. (Page 47).

National Runaway and Suicide Hotline, 24 hours a day
(800) 621-4000. (Page 47).

Runaway Hotline
(800) 231-6946; TX (800) 392-3352. (Page 47).

RUNAWAY SHELTERS

Children of the Night (pornography and prostitution)
(818) 908-4470; (800) 564-COTN (Page 48).

Covenant House
(800) 999-9999; (212) 330-0469. (Page 48).

Runaway Hotline
(800) 231-6946; TX (800) 392-3352. (Page 47).

Wyandotte House in Kansas
(913) 342-9332. (Page 48).

Youth Haven in Florida
(813) 774-2904; (813) 774-2698. (Page 48).

SAFETY

American Academy of Pediatrics Product Recommendations
(Page 18).

Child Safety Programs Handbook
(Page 23).

Food and Drug Safety
(Page 24).

Hug-A-Tree and Survive
(Page 19).

National Battery Ingestion Hotline
(202) 625-3333. (Page 20).

National Child Safety Council
(517) 764-6070. (Page 29).

National Safe Kids Campaign
(202) 939-4993. (Page 23).

National School Safety Center
(818) 377-6200. (Page 29).

Product Safety Hotline
(800) 638-2772; (800) 638-CPSC; (TTY) (800) 638-8270. (Page 18).

Safe Product Publications
(800) 638-2772. (Page 17).

Safe Toys and Sports Equipment
(800) 638-2772. (Page 17).

SCHIZOPHRENIA

Questions and Answers on Schizophrenia
(Page 104).

SCOLIOSIS

Scoliosis Association
(919) 846-2639. (Page 89).

SICKLE CELL DISEASE

National Association for Sickle Cell Disease
(800) 421-8453. (Page 74).

SKIN DISORDERS

Neurofibromatosis Foundation
(800) 323-7938; NY(212) 460-8980. (Page 90).

Skin Cancer Foundation
(212) 725-5176. (Page 89).

SMOKING

How To Stop Smoking
(Page 46).

SPACE

NASA Programs for Children
(Page 151).

SPEECH IMPAIRMENT

National Center for Stuttering
(800) 221-2483; (212) 532-1460. (Page 116).

National Council on Stuttering
(Page 116).

National Stuttering Project
(415) 566-5324. (Page 116).

Speak Easy International Foundation
(201) 262-0895. (Page 116).

SPINA BIFIDA

Spina Bifida Association of America
(800) 621-3141; (301) 770-7222. (Page 90).

SPORTS

AAU/USA Youth Sports Program
(317) 872-2900. (Page 143).

American College of Sports Medicine
(317) 637-9200. (Page 144).

Coaches' Program for Drug and Alcohol Prevention
(202) 307-7936. (Page 44).

Safe Sports Equipment
(800) 638-2772. (Page 17).

SPORTS FOR THE HANDICAPPED

Let's Play to Grow
(Page 144).

National Handicapped Sports
(301) 652-7505. (Page 113).

Special Olympics International
(202) 628-3630. (Page 107).

Special Recreation, Inc.
(319) 337-7578. (Page 113).

STEROIDS

Effects of Steroids
(Page 46).

SUDDEN INFANT DEATH

SIDS Alliance
(800) 221-7437; (301) 964-8000. (Page 91).

National Sudden Infant Death Syndrome Clearinghouse
(703) 821-8955. (Page 91).

SUICIDE

American Association of Suicidology
(303) 692-0985. (Page 53).

National Adolescent Hotline, 24-hour crisis intervention
(800) 621-4000. (Page 53).

Youth Suicide National Center
(415) 347-3961. (Page 53).

TELEVISION

Television Violence
(217) 384-1920. (Page 161).

Use and Abuse of TV Time
(612) 330-3300. (Page 162).

TOBACCO

How to Stop Smoking
(Page 46).

TOYS

Center for Special Education Technology
(Page 117).

Projects for Special Children (Clothing and Toys For Special Children)
(703) 549-2640. (Page 117).

Safe Toys
(800) 638-2772. (Page 17).

Toys For Special Children
(914) 478-0960. (Page 117).

TRANSPLANTS

Children's Transplant Association
(214) 287-8484. (Page 85).

Organ Donors
(800) 528-2971; (713) 961-9431. (Page 85).

United Network for Organ Sharing
(804) 330-8500. (Page 85).

TRANSPORTATION SAFETY

National Highway Traffic Safety Administration, Public Affairs
(800) 424-9393; (202) 366-0123 TTY (800) 434-9153; TTY (202) 755-8919. (Page 25).

Prevent Bicycle Accidents
(202) 366-2696. (Page 26).

Prevent Childhood Pedestrian Accidents
(202) 366-2696. (Page 26).

Safety Belts in School Buses
(800) 444-NHIF; (508) 485-9950. (Page 25).

TRAVEL

Instructions for Overseas Travel
(Page 153).

International Student Exchange, Youth for Understanding
(202) 966-6808; (800) TEENAGE. (Page 153).

Learning Geography
(Page 152).

Visiting our National Forests
(Page 145).

VENEREAL DISEASES

American Foundation for the Prevention of Venereal Disease
(212) 759-2069. (Page 51).

Contraceptive Use
(Page 50).

National Herpes Hotline
(919) 361-8488. (Page 51).

National Institute of Allergy and Infectious Diseases
(Page 51).

Sexually Transmitted Disease Hotline
(800) 227-8922. (Page 51).

Symptoms, Diagnosis, Treatment of Venereal Diseases
(Page 51).

VICTIMS

California Center on Victimology
(619) 235-4459. (Page 32).

Center for Democratic Renewal
(404) 221-0025. (Page 30).

Committee to Halt Useless College Killings
(516) 567-1130. (Page 30).

National Child Safety Council
(517) 764-6070. (Page 29).

National Organization for Victim Assistance (NOVA)
(202) 232-6682 (24 hour hotline). (Page 32).

National Victims Resource Center
(301) 251-5500. (Page 31).

Office of Victims of Crime, Department of Justice
(800) 627-6872. (Page 31).

Parents of Murdered Children & Other Survivors of Homicide Victims
(513) 721-5683. (Page 33).

VIOLENCE

Center for Democratic Renewal
(404) 221- 0025; (Page 30).

Committee to Halt Useless College Killings
516) 567-1130. (Page 30).

FBI, Office of Public Affairs
(Page 29).

Michigan Coalition Against Domestic Violence
(800) 333-7233. (Page 32).

National Coalition Against Domestic Violence
(202) 638-6388; TTY (202) 589-6671. (Page 31).

National Coalition on TV Violence
(217) 384-1920. (Page 161).

National Council on Child Abuse and Family Violence
(800) 222-2000; (202) 429-6695. (Page 32).

National Institute Against Prejudice and Violence
(301) 328-5170. (Page 30).

Office for Victims of Crime, Department of Justice
(800) 627-6872; (301) 251-5519. (Page 31).

Support for Children of Prisoners
(817) 531-1469. (Page 33).

VISUALLY IMPAIRED

National Association for Parents of the Visually Impaired
(800) 562-6265. (Page 120).

National Association for the Visually Handicapped
(212) 889-3141; (415) 221-8753 (western states). (Page 120).

National Society to Prevent Blindness
(800) 221-3004. (Page 121).

Retinitis Pigmentosa Foundation
(800) 638-2300; (301) 225-9400. (Page 121).

VOLUNTEERING

Peace Corps
(800) 424-8580, Ext. 2227. (Page 165).

WISH FULFILLMENT

Brass Ring Society
(800) 666-WISH; (913) 242-1666. (Page 92).

Camp Fantastic
(703) 667-3774. (Page 94).

Children's Wish Foundation International
(800) 323-9474. (Page 94).

Dream Factory
(800) 456-7556. (Page 93).

Dreams Come True
(904) 733-1010. (Page 94).

Grant-A-Wish Foundation of Maryland, The
(800) 933-5470; (301) 242-1549. (Page 92).

High Hopes Foundation of New Hampshire
(603) 898-5333. (Page 93).

Make-A-Wish Foundation of America
(602) 240-6600. (Page 93).

National Alliance of Wish Granting Organizations (NAGO)
(800) 666-WISH (Page 92).

Operation Liftoff
(215) 639-1586. (Page 94).

Starlight Foundation
(800) 274-7827; (213) 208-5885. (Page 93).

Sunshine Foundation
(800) 767-1976; (215) 335-2622. (Page 93).

Wish With Wings, A
(817) 469-9474; (708) 246-2723. (Page 94).

YOUTH EXCHANGE

Youth for Understanding
(800) TEENAGE; (202) 966-6808. **(Page 153).**

YOUTH ORGANIZATIONS

Big Brothers/Big Sisters of America
(215) 567-7000. **(Page 160).**

Boys and Girls Clubs of America
(212) 351-5900. **(Page 159).**

Boy Scouts of America
(214) 580-2000. **(Page 160).**

Girl Scouts of the U.S.A.
(212) 940-7500. **(Page 160).**

4-H Programs
(202) 447-5953. **(Page 160).**

National Future Farmers of America Organization
(703) 360-3600. **(Page 159).**

ALPHABETICAL INDEX OF ORGANIZATIONS THAT HELP CHILDREN

A

B

C

D

E

F

G

H

I

J

K

L

M

N

O

P

Q

R

S

T

U

V

W

Y

OTHER BOOKS TO HELP CHILDREN BY ROCKY RIVER PUBLISHERS

Order Form

Mail to ROCKY RIVER PUBLISHERS

P. O. BOX 1679, Shepherdstown, WV 25443

SHIP TO: Name:______________________________

Address:______________________________

City, State, Zip: ______________________________

Quantity	Description of Book	Price	Total Price
	HELP FOR CHILDREN	$10.95	
	STRESS STOPPERS	$6.95	
	MAC'S CHOICE	$8.95	
	MAC'S WORKBOOK	$3.50	
	MAC'S CHOICE POSTER	$6.50	
	S. S. FLASH CARDS	$8.95	
	Subtotal		
Applicable Tax (West Virginia residents, 6%)			
Shipping and Handling ($2.50 for first item and 50¢ for each additional item).			
THANK YOU FOR YOUR ORDER		TOTAL	

Method of Payment: Check VISA MasterCard (circle one)

Card Number ______________________. Expiration Date ____.

Signature ______________________.

Make checks payable to Rocky River Publishers and mail to the address above. **Phone orders call Toll-free** (800) 343-0686.